2199

3/99

EXECUTIVE
JETS

Geza Szurovy

MBI Publishing Company

First published in 1998 by MBI Publishing Company, 729 Prospect Avenue, PO Box 1, Osceola, WI 54020-0001 USA

MBI Publishing Company books are also available at discounts in bulk quantity for industrial or sales-promotional use. For details write to Special Sales Manager at Motorbooks International Wholesalers & Distributors, 729 Prospect Avenue, Osceola, WI 54020-0001 USA.

Library of Congress Cataloging-in-Publication Data Available

ISBN 0-7603-0558-7

On the front cover: Production of the G-IV SP replaced that of the standard G-IV in September 1992, offering even higher weights and improved payload range performance than its capable predecessor. *Paul Bowen*

On the frontispiece: Gulfstream claims that the G-V is the quietest aircraft in production. These passengers boarding for an overnight transpacific flight will easily be able to sleep on the way. *Gulfstream*

On the title page: The Challenger 600 challenged Gulfstream's dominance of the large executive jet market when it entered service in 1978. Its widebody cabin quickly gained followers. *Paul Bowen*

On the back cover: The typical G-V is configured for a flight crew of two and a passenger load of eight. Passengers have access to two galleys, a rest room with shower, five reclining seats, a three-seat couch that converts into a bed, a dining/conference area for four, and a business workstation with SATCOM, computer, and fax. Even the crew has their own restroom. *Paul Bowen*

Designed by Rebecca Allen

Printed in Hong Kong through World Print. Ltd.

CONTENTS

ACKNOWLEDGMENTS

A heavily illustrated book on executive jets would not have been possible without excellent photographs. The great majority of the photos presented here are the work of one photographer, Paul Bowen. In my mind Paul is the dean of general aviation photographers, who has done more than anyone else to soothe the aesthetic senses of those of us who think that viewing an airplane air-to-air is one of the most beautiful sights to behold. I would like to thank Paul for kindly providing many of the photos directly, and for taking many of the ones provided by (and credited to) the manufacturers. Paul is currently working on a comprehensive art photo book that will showcase his life's work with executive jets. I heartily encourage readers to keep an eye out for it.

I would also like to thank everyone at the various aircraft manufacturing companies and flight departments who were forthcoming with information, including Colin Clark for lending me a rare out-of-print history on Gulfstream. Every photo or piece of information is helpful in one way or another, and I appreciate it all.

Geza Szurovy

JET SET LIFTOFF

On September 4, 1957, the first Lockheed JetStar lifted off on its maiden flight, ushering in the era of the executive jet. Powered by two Bristol Siddeley Orpheus engines mounted aft, it was capable of whisking up to 10 passengers to their destination in pure jet comfort at three times the speed of any propeller-driven alternative. Following initial flight test, it went into production equipped with four Pratt & Whitney JT12A-8 Turbojets.

The Lockheed JetStar, first flown in 1957, was the first true executive jet, even though it was developed for the U.S. Air Force as a VIP transport. This is a late-model JetStar re-engined with Garrett TFE-731s. *Paul Bowen*

As with most "firsts," however, there are some differences of opinion regarding the JetStar's claim to being the first business jet, because it was originally developed as a VIP transport for the U.S. Air Force. Also claimed by some to be the first business jet is the smaller twin-engined North American Rockwell Saberliner which made its first flight in 1958. Designed as a low-cost USAF transport trainer, the T-39A was also destined to become a successful executive jet.

In an interesting early flirtation with the concept of the business jet, Beechcraft marketed a four-seat French civilian jet, the Morane-Saulnier Paris Jet, inspired by the Fouga Magister military trainer. It was more like a personal airplane—a jet-powered equivalent of Beechcraft's own Bonanza—but when Henry Timken, CEO of Timken Roller Bearing of Canton, Ohio, bought one in 1958, it was the first sale of a jet to a civilian buyer for business use. As Timken and his wife, both avid pilots, began tooling around in their personal jet for business and pleasure, several other efforts were underway to develop business jets.

At Britain's deHavilland a twin-engined executive jet was taking shape on paper by 1959, the

Dassault Aviation's Falcon 20 was derived from the Mystere fighter design. It first flew in 1963 and was selected by Pan American on the recommendation of Charles Lindbergh for its newly formed Business Jet Division. *Paul Bowen*

The first D.H.125, which became known as the Hawker, was one of the most successful midsized executive jets. It started life as a deHavilland, but by the time it first flew in 1962 the company had been merged into Hawker Siddeley.

D.H.125, so named because it was the company's 125th design. Its specs called for U.S. transcontinental capability at 435 knots, a stand-up cabin, and a lavatory. From a business standpoint it was a high risk project, with a hefty capital requirement and no assurance of a ready market. While an intercompany struggle to build the jet played itself out, deHavilland was merged into Hawker Siddeley. In 1961 the project got the go-ahead for an initial production of 30 aircraft when the Royal Air Force committed to buying 20 jets for navigational training. The D.H.125 first flew on August 13, 1962. Although the final design fell far short of U.S. transcontinental range, it was on its way to becoming the Hawker, one of the most successful business jets to date.

Across the channel from Hawker Siddeley another major aircraft maker, Dassault Aviation of France, was becoming interested in the concept of the business jet. Dassault, known for its Mirage and Mystere fighters, turned to its military jet experience to leapfrog some development requirements of a business jet. The company started with the Mystere fighter's wing and developed a business jet fuselage and empennage design for it. The result was the twin-engined Mystere XX which made its first flight on May 4, 1963. Its further refined production version, the Falcon 20, was to rival the Hawker in popularity.

These early business jets were large, expensive airplanes, purchased mostly by major corporations. A brilliant entrepreneurial avionics inventor derisively called them royal barges. His name was Bill Lear, and he concluded that what the market really needed was a small hot rod of a business jet that could offer jet airline performance at a fraction of the royal barges'

Bill Lear proudly holds up seven fingers for the first seven production Learjet 23s lined up behind him.

acquisition and operating costs. Although he never managed the development of an airplane, he won the Collier Trophy for a revolutionary autopilot design and was involved in modifying Lockheed Loadstar piston twins to improve their performance, and outfitting them as executive transports. So with characteristic élan he dove headlong into his Learjet dream.

Lear initially set up shop in Switzerland in 1958, having been inspired by the Swiss P.16 fighter for the Learjet's design, but relocated to Wichita in a huff when his Swiss employees insisted on lunch hours and weekends off. The airplane Lear and his designers created was as stunning in performance as it was in appearance and captured the public imagination like no other executive jet ever. Lear's talent for shameless self-promotion helped, but the airplane made "Learjet" the public's word for an executive jet on its own merit.

The Aero Commander was a direct competitor of the Learjet, certified only four months after the Lear 23. The aircraft shown is a Westwind, the Aero Commander's evolutionary descendant, at Meigs Field, Chicago. *Paul Bowen*

Frank Sinatra was an early customer. Arnold Palmer set a round-the-world record in one.

Only four months behind the Learjet was Aero Commander's Jet Commander, an unglamorous, blunt-nosed, mid-winged, businesslike machine that performed as well as the Learjet and carved out its own respectable share of the light-jet market.

The increasing demand for executive aircraft also caught the attention of the Grumman Corporation of Bethpage, New York. Grumman, looking to diversify from its total dependence on military contracts, chose the turboprop alternative and entered the market with the Gulfstream I. The G-I first flew in 1959 and became a popular executive workhorse. It was sufficiently economical and unglamorous enough to be available even to middle-level managers of many of the companies that operated them, and was often used as a corporate shuttle between company facilities. In executive configuration it seated 10 to 12 passengers, but in shuttle mode it could be configured for up to 24.

There was much debate about just how large the market would be for executive jets, and the industry was especially vulnerable to business cycles, but as the 1960s progressed, there was room for every well managed and well capitalized player. The Falcon 20 acquired an aura of glamour when, on Charles Lindbergh's recommendation, the then high-flying Pan American Airways selected it as the sole airplane for its newly established Business Jets Division.

The Learjets, Commanders, Hawkers, and Falcons were so well received that Grumman realized there was room at the top to provide an in-house option for its Gulfstream I operators who were ready to move up to jets. The result was the Gulfstream II, the first transcontinental business jet that captured the imagination of Fortune 500 CEOs as much as the Learjet mesmerized the general public.

The Gulfstream II was the ultimate royal barge, but as the 1960s were coming to a close the biggest executive jet success story was about to get underway at the light end of the market. Jets weren't the only business airplanes rapidly gaining popularity. High-end piston twins and twin turboprops were also filling a large demand. King among them was Beechcraft's King Air, the Rolls Royce of turboprops. In the spirit of the time

the jet makers were forever striving to make their swept-wing creations go faster, higher, farther. They had no time for the turboprop pilot dreading the huge step up into "hot" jets. And therein Cessna Aircraft saw a big opportunity.

Why not make a tame, straight-winged jet that handsomely outflew the turboprops but was docile enough for turboprop pilots to fly with little additional training? Cessna was not as new to jets as it may seem, having designed and built over 1,200 T-37 primary jet trainers for the U.S. Air Force, a project that started in 1954. Cessna's entry-level business jet was announced in 1968 as the Fanjet 500. By 1969 it was called the Citation, and on September 15 of that year it flew for the first time, equipped with the Pratt & Whitney JT15D-1 fanjet engine.

Those who marveled at how Cessna could score a home run by building a jet that was *slower* than the competition didn't get it. The other business jets were not the Citation's competition when it was launched.

A fascinating portrait of the executive jet world in the mid-1960s at the Indianapolis race track. Upper center is a Gulfstream II, to its right in the back row is a Gulfstream I turboprop, a Hawker HS125, a North American Rockwell Saberliner, and in the front row are Learjets, Learjets, and more Learjets—visible proof of Bill Lear's perception of what the market wanted.

The Cessna Fanjet mockup in 1968. The airplane was astutely aimed at the performance gap between the turboprops and the jets at the time. When it entered service as the Citation 500, it went on to unprecedented success in the executive jet market. *Cessna*

It was filling a void between turboprops and jets in which there was *no* competition. Buyers flocked to the docile entry-level jet, but that was not all. As the needs of Citation customers grew, Cessna grew with them, bringing out increasingly capable Citations. Most popular among them was the Citation II. The straight-wing Citations proved so easy to fly that the FAA even granted single pilot authorization to several of them.

By 1979 Cessna was ready to up the ante to the midsized, swept-wing, stand-up cabin Citation III. The company soon took a comfortable lead in number of business jets made by any manufacturer, and in 1997 it sold the 2,500th Citation. It was a highly swept-wing Mach .92 Citation X, the fastest business jet in the world, an age beyond the Fanjet 500.

One of the most significant developments of the late 1960s was the introduction of the high bypass fanjet engine suitable for business jets. It dramatically decreased fuel consumption and improved performance, and none too soon in light of the oil crisis of 1973 that saw a quadrupling of fuel prices. Most

Left
The Gulfstream II, which was introduced in 1966, had the large transcontinental business jet market to itself for over two decades. *Paul Bowen*

15

The Citation I. When the Citation entered service in 1972, it was known as the Citation 500. A minor power upgrade soon thereafter resulted in a name change to the Citation I. *Paul Bowen*

A Learjet 25 refurbished in the 1990s for a California winery by Duncan Aviation, an independent completion center in Lincoln, Nebraska. Inside, a special cabinet was created to showcase the winery's best vintages. *Duncan Aviation*

notable was the Garrett (now AlliedSignal) TFE731 that powers more executive jets in its different variations than any other engine.

Manufacturers switched to the fanjets with enthusiasm. Among some of the most popular fanjets that made their appearance during the 1970s were Learjet's Lear 35 and the stand-up cabin Lear 55, the Lear 28 (the first civilian jet to feature winglets), the Citations, the Westwind (successor to the Aero Commander), the Falcon 20F, the Falcon 10 (a smaller stablemate of the Falcon 20), and the Hawker 700.

Many older model executive jets received a new lease on life when re-engined with Garret TFE731s by aftermarket conversion companies such as AiResearch. Among the types so modified were JetStars, Saberliners, Hawkers, and Falcon 20s.

Another significant development of the late 1970s was the challenge of the Gulfstream II's supremacy by two large executive jets, the sleek, three-engined Falcon 50, and the Canadair Challenger 600. Both airplanes provided transcontinental range. The Challenger 600 was based on the Learstar 600 design, bought by the Canadian government-

The cockpit of a 1970s Learjet 35 looks outdated by 1990s glass cockpit standards. Great strides have also been made in upholstery since this airplane entered service.

The Learjet 35's high bypass Garrett TFE731 fanjet represented a major advance in jet engine technology. It greatly reduced fuel consumption and increased performance compared to the low bypass engine. *Paul Bowen*

owned Canadair from Bill Lear, but modified practically beyond recognition. In spite of falling slightly short of original range predictions (a problem addressed on subsequent models), it gained quick acceptance for its widebody cabin, which was by far the biggest interior among executive jets.

Gulfstream, by now independent of Grumman, introduced the Gulfstream III, successor to the venerable G-II. It featured a new wing with winglets, a larger fuselage, and a greater fuel load. Interestingly enough, it retained the original low bypass Spey engines but could fly 3,600 nm, a gain of 1,000 nm over the G-II, and could do so at a higher cruise speed.

The 1980s saw the spread of highly integrated glass cockpits in executive jets and the appearance of full authority digital engine control (FADEC), which controls the engine by wire, sending instructions through highly sophisticated computer processors instead of mechanical linkages. It also saw the emergence of several exciting new models that are still in production today, among them the Astra, Israel Aircraft Industries' first homegrown jet following its acquisition of the Westwind. These aircraft are covered in detail in subsequent chapters.

In 1985 Beechcraft finally entered the executive jet business by buying the Mitsubishi Diamond II production line and upgrading the airplane to the Beechjet 400. The company would add to its jet line-up in the 1990s by acquiring the Hawker line from British Aerospace.

Some of the excitement in the executive jet industry during the 1980s wasn't because of the airplanes but with the business fortunes of the companies. Cessna was, by then, owned by Textron and Beechcraft was bought by Raytheon.

Learjet almost went out of business during the recession at the beginning of the 1980s. At the same time the Canadian government was grappling with a whopping $2.4 billion loss of taxpayer's money on the mismanaged Canadair Challenger program. Salvation for both companies ultimately came from Bombardier which acquired them and orchestrated their recovery

and made them an integral part of its thriving aerospace business established through skillful acquisitions.

Lee Iacocca, CEO of the Chrysler Corporation, was so enamored by his Gulfstream that he convinced Chrysler to buy the company. When Chrysler decided to concentrate on core businesses a few years later, it sold Gulfstream to the Forstmann Little Group, one of Wall Street's most successful leveraged buyout firms that eventually took the company into the ultra-long-range jet era.

While the ride was wild at times, in the long run the executive jet industry has been a remarkable success story, and the trend continues. After a scary start in the aftermath of the 1987 stock market crash, the 1990s turned into a boom time for executive jets. The manufacturing of established models rose sharply. Significant

Executive jet ownership twenty-first-century style. The three types of aircraft offered by Business JetSolution's FlexJets fractional ownership program. In the back is a Challenger 604; to the right is a Learjet 60; in front is a Learjet 31A. Fractional owners buy a fraction of one jet in a pool of jets and have access to any of the pool airplanes for an allotted amount of annual flight time. *Bombardier*

technological progress was made in airframe and avionics technology, and more all-new models made it onto the drawing board.

Perhaps most significant is that to a greater extent than ever before, executive jets have gained wide acceptance as essential business tools instead of expensive perks. In the drive toward increasing efficiency and productivity, fractional ownership, a new form of ownership that allows a buyer to own a fraction of a jet for a fraction of the total cost, has been pioneered by Richard Santulli's Executive Jet Aviation (EJA).

Under its NetJets program EJA manages a vast fleet of executive jets, all identical within a particular type, any one of which is available to any fractional owner up to the limits of the owner's annual flight time entitlement. The program has been so successful that it has made EJA one of the biggest executive jet fleet buyers in history and has spawned numerous competitors.

The growing challenges of globalization are continuing to increase demand for the services of business jets worldwide, and open up exciting new markets for them. The following chapters delve in detail into these exciting aircraft currently in production and under development.

The midsized swept-wing Citation III was a quantum leap for Cessna, in line with the company's strategy to have an airplane ready for owners of the smaller Citations who were ready to move up. *Paul Bowen*

N106CJ

2

LIGHT JETS

Light jets are generally considered to be executive jets that have a range of 1,000 nm to 2,000 nm, carry five to eight passengers besides the pilots, and have a price tag (as of 1998) of approximately $3.5 to $8 million. Because of their relatively low price (in jet terms) for the performance they deliver, they are the most numerous in the executive jet market.

The CitationJet was the first of the lightest jets made possible by the small, light, and powerful Williams-Rolls FJ44 engine developed from the powerplant powering the Tomahawk cruise missile. The acquisition and operating costs of the CitationJet and its peers are competitive with turboprops. They can be flown by a single pilot. Going to

There is a wide range of capabilities and performance within the category among current production models. The most recent technological development has been the emergence of new aircraft at the lightest end of the market, such as the Cessna CitationJet, the Raytheon Premiere I, and the Sino Swearingen SJ30, all designed to compete with turboprops such as the King Air and Pilatus PC-12.

These new jets were made possible by the introduction of an innovative low-cost jet engine, the Williams-Rolls FJ44, which provides 1,900 to 2,200 pounds of thrust and delivers pure jet performance at turboprop economics.

The most innovative entrant at the lightest end of the field is the VisionAire Vantage, a composite six-seat, 350-knot airplane powered by a single Pratt &

The Citation Bravo is the successor of the highly popular Citation II, featuring a 10-percent gain in power and a 15-percent gain in fuel efficiency. *Cessna*

The Citation Ultra is the highest performance straight-wing Citation with a maximum cruise speed of 430 knots and a reach of 1,800 nm. *Cessna*

Whitney JT15D-5 engine. Increasing acceptance of high-cost singles and easing regulations that govern their commercial use bode well for the Vantage.

At the other end of the spectrum are the light jets that are really midsized in practically every respect except price, such as the Bombardier Learjet 45 and this category's only jet with a stand-up cabin, the Cessna Citation Excel. In the middle are such workhorses as the Citation Bravo and Ultra, the Learjet 31A, and the Beechjet 400A.

Cessna CitationJet

The smallest jet in the Citation line, the Citation-Jet, is aimed at the owner-pilot who is keener to do the flying from the left front seat than ride in the back. In the Cessna tradition it is one of several Citations certified to be flown by a single pilot.

The CitationJet was the launch customer for the Williams-Rolls FJ44-1 engine, a breakthrough in efficiency that for the first time makes light pure jets competitive with turboprops. One of the lesser

The Citation Ultra's sumptuous cabin makes maximum use of the space available. *Cessna*

known benefits of the end of the Cold War, the FJ44 came about as the result of cutbacks in defense budgets that prompted Williams Research, America's largest maker of jet engines for cruise missiles, to seek civilian opportunities. The company teamed up with Rolls Royce to develop the Williams-Rolls FJ44 turbofan engine. The Citation Jet's FJ44-1 provides 1,900 pounds of thrust, weighs considerably less than the Citation I's original Pratt & Whitney, burns less fuel, and is less expensive.

The FJ44 engines look small compared to the ones usually hung on business jets. Key to each engine's light weight is that it contains fewer than 700 components compared to about 2,500 in the typical earlier generation business jet engine. The most novel reduction in the number of engine components was achieved in the turbine fan and two compressor rotors.

The Citation Excel's state-of-the-art cockpit features a Honeywell Primus 1000 avionics suite. *Cessna*

Each is precision milled out of a single block of metal, blades and all, instead of assembled from countless individual blades produced separately. Damaged blades are reparable in place; a component need not be discarded because of a nick in a blade.

Also contributing to the CitationJet's light weight are thrust attenuators, used instead of the heavier thrust reversers, one for each engine. They look like black paddles flush with the engines and extend aft. On the ground, when power is reduced to idle, they are designed to automatically swing outward, deflecting any thrust and providing braking action.

That the high tech CitationJet flies faster and higher than a contending turboprop is no big surprise, but that it does so on less fuel and has a competitive purchase price is a breakthrough accomplishment. The CitationJet's exceptionally efficient,

A good illustration of the comfort provided by the Excel's stand-up cabin, unique among light jets. *Cessna*

The Citation Excel delivers Ultra performance and a stand-up cabin for a slightly higher price. *Cessna*

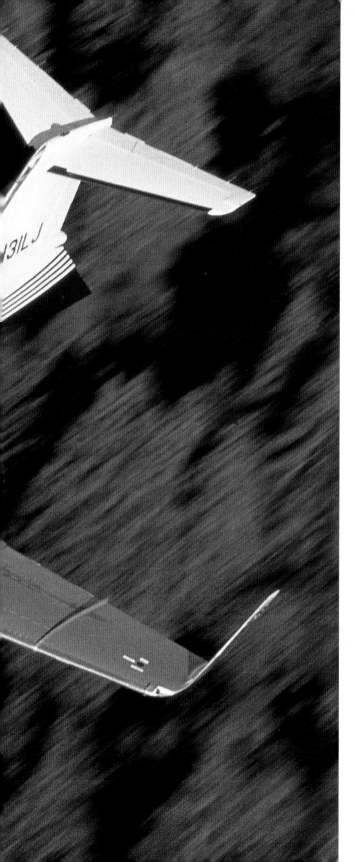

natural laminar flow wing jointly developed by Cessna and NASA has contributed greatly to this feat, giving the Citation engineers exactly what they wanted for a follow-up to the Citation I. The CitationJet's wing retains laminar airflow along the entire first third of its surface, compared to a nominal amount on more conventional wings. Simply put, laminar flow is super-smooth, unruffled airflow, which adheres to the wing's surface. It makes the wing more efficient because it creates much less drag than even slightly disturbed airflow. Most of the CitationJet's wing skin is bonded. The few rivets used are aft, completely faired in, and invisible.

Gone from the wing's leading edge are the traditional, pneumatically-pulsing, black rubber deicing boots, which would have made laminar flow impossible. Instead there are two stationary polished metal strips perfectly faired into the rest of the wing. Bleed air drawn from the engine at 330 degrees Fahrenheit is channeled along these strips, making short work of any ice accumulation. During the certification process, 6 inches of ice was allowed to build up along the leading edge before being zapped with bleed air. The ice melted in record time.

The cockpit is laid out with the single pilot in mind. Most switches and controls are clustered around the left seat but are also within reasonable reach of the optional copilot. The visibility from the cockpit is excellent, providing an impressive 340-degree field of vision.

Although not the first light jet to be equipped with digital multifunction displays, the CitationJet was a leader for its size in making the switch from analog displays. A Honeywell SPZ-5000 avionics suite is standard. It includes two Electronic Flight Instrument System (EFIS) displays on the pilot's side. EFIS capability for the copilot is optional. A Global Wulfsberg GNS-X unit manages navigation, integrating several information sources, including GPS.

The Learjet 31 combined the longhorn wing of the Learjet 55 with the cabin of the Learjet 35. The resulting entry-level Learjet was as easy to fly as any executive jet yet retained traditional Learjet performance. *Bombardier*

The CitationJet has considerable range and load bearing for an airplane its size. Typically, four passengers and one pilot can go approximately 1,500 miles at a high cruise of up to 380 knots with 45-minute reserves. That translates into such distances as Chicago–Phoenix, Denver–Tampa, and Seattle–Minneapolis with flight times of around three and a half hours. The little jet is most in its element between 31,000 and 41,000 feet.

CITATIONJET VITAL STATISTICS

Powerplants	Williams-Rolls FJ44-1
Thrust per engine	1,900 lbs
Seats	6 to 7
Max. takeoff weight	10,400 lbs
Max. useful load	4,185 lbs
Max. cruise speed	380 kts
Range (45-min reserves)	1,485 nm
FAA certified altitude	41,000 ft

Cessna Citation Bravo

The Citation Bravo is the successor to Cessna's popular Citation II. It neatly fills the niche between the smaller CitationJet and the larger, more expensive Citation Ultra. Powered by the Pratt & Whitney PW530A engine that delivers 2,885 pounds of thrust per side, it gains 10 percent in power and 15 percent in fuel efficiency over the JT15D-4-powered Citation II.

The increased power, combined with the cleaned-up Citation II-SP wing, yielded a maximum cruise speed that exceeded Cessna's forecast of 394 knots and made the straight-winged Bravo a 400-plus-knot airplane by. This is a great achievement given its predecessors' reputation for being on the slow side in jet terms.

The Bravo was first flown in 1994, and customer deliveries commenced in 1997. At its maximum takeoff weight of 14,800 pounds it can climb directly to 41,000 feet in 28 minutes. It continues the Citation tradition of being an outstanding short field performer by routinely operating into airfields with runways under 3,000 feet. The Bravo can carry up to eight passengers and has a full-cabin-width aft lavatory, a feature that is becoming a standard requirement in all but the lightest jets. Its maximum range is 1,600 nm with four passengers and NBAA (National Business Aircraft Association) IFR reserves.

A small but significant improvement over the Citation II is the Bravo's trailing link landing gear that makes it easier to accomplish smooth touch-

This Learjet 31A was one of the first business jets delivered to Eastern Europe when it was purchased by a Czech pulp and paper mill manufacturer. *Bombardier*

The Learjet 45, certified in 1997, carries eight to nine passengers. It is a 100-percent-new airplane, one of the first "paperless" designs developed entirely on computers. *Bombardier*

downs instead of what are euphemistically referred to as "firm arrivals."

The Bravo's avionics suite features the Honeywell P-1000 digital flight guidance system with pilot's and copilot's primary flight displays and a multifunction display. Flight management is accomplished by an Allied Signal GNS-XI which includes GPS and VNAV (vertical navigation).

CITATION BRAVO VITAL STATISTICS

Powerplants	Pratt & Whitney PW530A
Thrust per engine	2,885 lbs
Seats	8
Max. takeoff weight	14,800 lbs
Max. useful load	6,250 lbs
Max. cruise speed	401 kts
Range (45-min reserves)	1,900 nm
FAA certified altitude	45,000 ft

Cessna Citation Ultra

As Cessna's Citation line achieved its goal of providing an incremental transition up from turboprops, for a growing segment of established Citation operators the comparison was no longer with the slower turboprops but with other faster executive jets. If the straight-wing Citation was to sustain its dominant position, it had to become a faster airplane.

Rather than opt for a swept wing to increase speed, Cessna put the line's light and easy-to-manufacture straight wing on a drag reduction diet and equipped the new models with higher thrust versions of the Pratt & Whitney engines. This approach yielded handsome dividends.

The Ultra is the highest performance "straight" wing Citation, the first in its line capable of exceeding its maximum Mach operating limit in level flight. It is also one of the finest examples of the good job Cessna has done developing the Citation line to match the expanding needs of its customer base.

On first blush the Ultra looks like a little Citation from the early 1970s that has grown up, and indeed, it has. All the evolutionary improvements and refinements that have been incorporated into the straight-wing Citation line over the years converge in the Ultra. Its fuselage is 5 feet longer than the original Citation, the result of two fuselage stretches: 3.5 feet on the Citation II and an additional 1.5 feet on the later model Citation V. It has the substantially redesigned wing developed for the Citation S/II and also used on the Citation V, which significantly reduced cruise drag and contributed to an increase in cruise speed. It is powered by the Pratt & Whitney JT15D-5D engine, the most powerful version of the JT15D used on several other straight-wing Citations and which produces 3,045 pounds of thrust per side. Its Honeywell Primus 1000 EFIS avionics system and Global GNS-X flight management system are state of the art.

The net result is a very capable and versatile executive jet. It can carry eight passengers in its cabin in a double club seating arrangement at cruise speeds consistently reaching 430 knots. It has a maximum certified ceiling of 45,000 feet and range of up to 1,800 nm. Like all the straight-wing Citations, it is certified for single-pilot operation. It also has a full-cabin-width aft lavatory.

The Learjet 45 is made with heavy use of computer-aided manufacturing at various Bombardier locations. Its fuselage is made in Belfast, the wings in Toronto, with overall production and assembly in Wichita. *Bombardier*

The Ultra has proved to be as popular with corporate owners and individual operators as its predecessors. And for those who can't justify owning an entire aircraft, it was made available at a fraction of its total cost through the NetJets fractional ownership program of Executive Jet Aviation. EJA's purchase of 25 Ultras was the largest executive jet order in history at the time. (EJA has since exceeded this record with other massive orders for a variety of executive jets.)

The Ultra's airframe has a number of noteworthy features. Bonding is used heavily throughout to achieve a super-smooth, low drag finish. A sweptwing root and gap seals between the ailerons and flaps result in further drag reduction. The ailerons and the two-panel Fowler flaps are made of composite material, yielding a considerable savings in weight. There are two cavernous baggage compartments, one aft and one in the nose. Both pass the multiple golf bag test with flying colors, and the rear compartment also has a ski-tube option. The Ultra's weight and balance range is so wide that it is practically impossible to inadvertently load it out of limits under any scenario.

The JT15D-5D engines, which produce 3,045 pounds of thrust each, benefit from an important technological improvement. Unlike earlier versions used on the Citation V, which have separate individual blades slotted around a disk, the -5D's fan and compressor are each milled from a single piece of solid metal. The closer production tolerances made possible by the new milling process, together with a redesigned, higher performance fan-blade airfoil and other design changes have increased the engine's thrust by 145 pounds and improved fuel efficiency.

The Ultra retains the immense cockpit-side windows of the straight-winged Citation line. They come way down to elbow level, providing superior visibility. The three huge EFIS displays of the Primus 1000 avionics system are also a pilot's delight. Measuring 8x7 inches, they are the largest EFIS screens to be found in executive jets in the Ultra's class and provide an exceptionally uncluttered display.

In high-speed cruise at 45,000 feet, under standard conditions, the Ultra's maximum range with five passengers is 1,800 nm with 45-minute fuel reserves achieved in a flight time of 4 hours and 35 minutes.

Raytheon's Beechjet 400A was derived from the Mitsubishi Diamond II which Raytheon Aircraft (then Beechcraft) bought in 1985 to gain instant entry into executive jet production. *Raytheon*

On the typically shorter legs of most executive trips it can easily carry a full complement of eight passengers with room to spare, even with the more stringent NBAA IFR fuel reserve criteria.

CITATION ULTRA VITAL STATISTICS

Powerplants	Pratt & Whitney JT15D-5D
Thrust per engine	3,045 lbs
Seats	6 to 9
Max. takeoff weight	16,300 lbs
Max. useful load	6,850 lbs
Max. cruise speed	430 kts
Range (45-min reserves)	1,800 nm
FAA certified altitude	45,000 ft

Cessna Citation Excel

One persistent drawback to light executive jets over the years was that none of them had a stand-up cabin. That changed when Cessna unveiled a new addition to its prolific Citation line, the Citation Excel. First announced at the National Business Aviation Association's 1994 convention, it flew its initial flight in February 1996 and was certified in April 1998.

In the Excel, Cessna brought together the high end of its light-jet line with a fuselage rooted in the company's midsize aircraft. The fuselage is virtually the same length as that of the Citation VII, and its cross-section is exactly the same as the Citation X. An under-fuselage wing carry-through configuration allows the cabin's dropped aisle to extend all the way aft, opening into a spacious lavatory behind which is a clothes closet suitable for hanging suits.

The rest of the airframe has much in common with the Citation Ultra including the high performance straight wing featuring sweptwing roots and the cruciform tail. One feature not retained from the Ultra is its stiff landing gear, replaced by the much more forgiving trailing link gear. In the cockpit the Excel is practically identical to the Ultra, equipped with the same Honeywell Primus 1000 avionics suite.

The Excel put on some weight during the development process, but at its 20,000-pound maximum takeoff weight and with a VFR range of 2,027 nm in normal cruise with four passengers onboard, it still qualifies as a light jet, albeit at the high end.

To deliver Ultra performance with the added weight imposed by the larger fuselage, the Excel is powered by two Pratt & Whitney PW 545A engines that deliver 3,640 pounds of thrust each. The power gain represents an increase of 595 pounds per engine over the Ultra's Pratt & Whitney JT15D-5D.

The airframe-engine combination enables the Excel at its maximum takeoff weight to climb to 43,000 feet in 25 minutes and cruise at speeds of up to 430 knots, matching the Ultra. In range the Excel has a slight advantage.

The Learjet 45's Honeywell Primus 1000 avionics suite includes an electronic instrument and crew alerting system (EICAS). *Bombardier*

CITATION EXCEL VITAL STATISTICS

Powerplants	Pratt & Whitney PW 545A
Thrust per engine	3,640 lbs
Seats	7 to 9
Max. takeoff weight	20,000 lbs
Max. useful load	6,500 lbs
Max. cruise speed	430 kts
Range (45-min reserves)	2,027 nm
FAA certified altitude	45,000 ft

Bombardier Learjet 31A

The Learjet 31A (and its earlier version the Lear 31) is Bombardier's entry-level executive jet, certified in 1991, prior to Learjet's acquisition by Bombardier. Its design objective was to combine traditional Learjet speed with solid short-field capability and good fuel economy to carry seven passengers and a crew of two in great comfort at one of the most economical operating costs for a light jet. It was also designed to be exceptionally docile to lay to rest any lingering notions from the early days that Learjets were hot.

The 31A has its roots in the Model 35's fuselage and Garrett (now Allied Signal) turbofan engines that deliver 3,500 pounds of thrust each and in the larger Model 55's super-efficient, high aspect ratio "longhorn" wing, so named because of its vortex-reducing winglets' visual effect.

Great effort went into refining the 31A's aerodynamic details to minimize drag and optimize handling characteristics. The result is an airplane that can routinely operate out of fields as short as 3,000 feet, quickly blast up to the most fuel efficient altitudes (as high as 51,000 feet), and race at high speed and low fuel burn to its destination as far away as 1,266 nm with IFR reserves and about 1,500 nm in VFR weather.

The Learjet 31A's main improvement over the Model 31 is its glass cockpit. A Bendix/King five-tube EFIS 50 electronic display system driven by three symbol generators provides five digital displays which replace traditional analog instruments except for the engine gauges and a few emergency standby items. Dual central air data computers (ADCs) with digitally interfaced displays provide altitude and airspeed information and dual attitude heading reference systems (AHRS) replace the artificial horizon and heading

One of the most interesting technological developments of the 1990s was the introduction of automatically woven composite fuselage construction on the Raytheon Premiere I light jet. *Raytheon*

gyros. The information, however, is still presented in traditional fashion on separate single purpose displays instead of integrated into one primary flight display as is the case with subsequent generations of glass cockpits. In addition, the company put exceptional effort into refining the superb Bendix/King KFC 3100 autopilot/flight director, which is full integrated with the airplane's state-of-the-art navigation system.

The Learjet 31A lives up to the line's reputation for exceptional performance. At its 16,750-pound maximum gross weight it can carry a useful load of 5,985 pounds under most conditions. This amounts to seven passengers, their bags, and a full fuel load of 4,124 pounds (615 gallons). And the ride is more like flying a Northrop T-38 than an executive jet. Acceleration on takeoff is legendary; climb performance is exceptional, and unlike some of its competitors that can barely struggle up to 51,000 feet, the Lear 31A can routinely operate at this height in great economy at speeds up to Mach .81.

Handling is also exceptional at the low end of the envelope. As the wings exceed critical angle of attack in the stall, the horizontal stabilizer and delta fins in the rear go to work. Set at a lower angle of attack than the wings, they continue to generate lift when the

Raytheon's fiber placement system in action, weaving the carbon fiber fuselage of the Premiere I. *Raytheon*

wings no longer do, causing the rear of the airplane to rise and the nose to pitch down.

The Federal Aviation Administration was sufficiently impressed with the 31A's stall characteristics to certify it without requiring a stick pusher found in most transport category aircraft, which automatically slams the control column forward to initiate stall recovery if a stall is allowed to develop in spite of the stick shaker's warnings.

BOMBARDIER LEARJET 31A
VITAL STATISTICS

Powerplants	AlliedSignal TFE 731-2
Thrust per engine	3,500 lbs
Seats (excluding crew)	7 to 9
Max. takeoff weight	16,750 lbs
Max. useful load	5,985 lbs
Max. cruise speed	Mach .81
Range (IFR)	1,266 nm
FAA certified altitude	51,000 ft

Bombardier Learjet 45

The Learjet 45 was a 100-percent-new Learjet and one of the first executive jets to be a paperless design, developed entirely on computers. It is also a technology leader because it also was built almost entirely by computer-aided machinery. This high-tech approach has yielded unprecedented efficiencies for Learjet, enabling the company to meet its design objectives of providing a larger, more comfortable cabin environment at a highly competitive price without sacrificing traditional Learjet performance.

When the company began the development of the 45, it started with the cabin, going through five fuselage mockups to establish the market's needs. The result was a noncircular cabin cross-section with room for double club seating and a flat floor (no dropped center aisle) to maximize legroom for seated passengers. Another important feature is a roomy aft lavatory.

To keep the airplane's purchase price and operating costs at economical levels, exceptional effort was exerted to optimize the aerodynamic characteristics of the airframe. With NASA's cooperation an airfoil was defined that has substantially improved drag characteristics at transonic cruise speeds. This makes higher speed cruise possible at higher altitudes on the same amount of power that propels aircraft of lesser performance, at a higher level of economic efficiency. The wing was optimized for cruise at Mach .81. The Learjet 45 can attain this speed by climbing directly to an initial cruise altitude of 45,000 feet after a maximum gross-weight takeoff. As fuel burns off, the airplane can climb to as high as 51,000 feet.

To enhance low-speed handling the wing incorporates a leading edge shaped for maximum lift at low speed and a -3-degree twist and drooped leading edge outboard for good stall characteristics. Stall behavior is also aided by the delta fins similar to the ones on other Learjets of more recent vintage and retrofittable to the Learjet 35. The advanced design makes complex lift generating devices unnecessary. The Learjet 45 is equipped only with simple flaps, and all control linkages are mechanical and unboosted.

Learjet's acquisition by Bombardier, Inc. in 1990 was a major shot in the arm, ensuring Learjet's survival and making possible the development of the Learjet 45. The association with Bombardier also provided opportunities for optimum sourcing of components from within Bombardier's vast network of aircraft manufacturing operations. The Learjet 45's wings are made in Toronto, the wings in Belfast, and assembly and overall project control is in Wichita.

Power is provided by two FADEC controlled AlliedSignal TFE 731-20 engines providing 3,500 pounds of thrust each. The Learjet 45 has a VFR range of 2,200 nm and an NBAA IFR range of 1,710 nm with four passengers onboard. Honeywell's Primus 1000 avionics suite provides flight and navigation information including an engine information and crew alerting system (EICAS) on four 8x7-inch flat panel screens.

The Learjet 45 made its maiden flight on October 7, 1995, 32 years to the day after the first flight of the first Learjet, the Model 23.

Completed Raytheon Premiere I carbon fiber forward fuselage shell. *Raytheon*

BOMBARDIER LEARJET 45 VITAL STATISTICS

Powerplants	AlliedSignal TFE 730-20
Thrust per engine	3,500 lbs
Seats	8 to 9
Max. takeoff weight	20,200 lbs
Max. useful load	7,600 lbs
Max. cruise speed	Mach .81/463 kts
Range (45-minute reserves)	2,200 nm
FAA certified altitude	51,000 ft

Raytheon Beechjet 400A

In the early 1980s Beechcraft began to seriously focus on the long standing problem of losing King Air turboprop customers when they traded up to a pure jet. Rather than go through the development of a pure jet of its own from scratch, the company decided to leapfrog the process by acquiring the MU 300 Diamond business jet program from Japan's Mitsubishi Corporation.

The original Diamond was slightly underpowered with its Pratt & Whitney JT15D-4 engines, especially hampering its operations from high altitude airports in hot conditions. By the time Beechcraft acquired the program in 1985, Mitsubishi was completing development of the Diamond II, re-engined with the more powerful JT15D-5 engines that produced 2,900 pounds of thrust each and cured the Diamond I's shortage of power.

Beechcraft made further refinements to the Diamond II, including making an optional 100-gallon fuselage fuel tank standard and equipping the airplane with Rohr thrust reversers. The airplane made its Beechcraft debut in 1986 as the Beechjet 400.

In 1991 the airplane became the Beechjet 400A when it received a major upgrade with the installation of a Collins Pro Line 4 avionics suite, the first glass cockpit in a light jet that fully integrated all flight information into one primary flight display (PFD). The certified ceiling was increased from 41,000 feet to 45,000 feet. The fuselage fuel tank was relocated in the belly of the aircraft to provide room in the already spacious cabin for moving the lavatory aft. The interior was also redesigned. With these modifications the Beechjet matured into an outstanding step-up choice for King Air owners and attracted a loyal following in its own right.

Beechjet owners especially like two features about the airplane that distinguished it from its peers when it was introduced: its spacious cabin and its high cruise speed. The cabin has an oval shape that gives it greater height in relation to width. This rewards seated passengers with more head and shoulder room than what is available in comparable aircraft with circular fuselage cross-sections. Its typical cruise speed of Mach .76 can

true out as high as 450 knots under certain conditions, and it can attain its maximum Mach operating speed of .78 in level flight.

The Beechjet owes its high speed in part to its sophisticated, highly swept wings. At low speeds, however, the highly loaded swept wings run out of lift sooner than desired, a problem for which the designers came up with a solution unique to the airplane among executive jets. The Beechjet has no ailerons. Roll control is achieved, instead, by full-span, narrow chord spoilers. This leaves the entire trailing edge available for double-slotted Fowler flaps which reduce landing speeds to acceptable levels, keeping the Beechjet competitive at the low-speed range of the envelope.

The spoilers give the airplane a heavier feel in roll than the typical light jet, making it similar to larger transport category aircraft. This was one reason why the U.S. Air Force selected it as the training aircraft for its Tanker Transport Trainer System (TTTS) program. The TTTS contract meant an order of over 200 Beechjets for the company. The military designation for the TTTS aircraft is T-1A Jayhawk. The first Jayhawk entered service as a Beechcraft, but by the time the last one was delivered, the company had become Raytheon Aircraft.

For Beechjet pilots the biggest treat of the 400A when it came out was the Collins Pro Line 4 glass cockpit (mentioned above). Three tubes were standard, but many operators chose the optional four-tube system that gives each pilot his or her own independently-driven primary flight display (PFD) and multi-function display (MFD).

With its exceptionally comfortable cabin and well equipped cockpit the seven- or eight-seat Beechjet 400A can carry four passengers 1,550 nm with NBAA IFR reserves in standard conditions in maximum range cruise. Its VFR reach in maximum range cruise with four passengers is 1,900 nm.

The Premiere I is Raytheon's very light jet, powered by the Williams-Rolls FJ44-2 engine. Note the resemblance of certain elements of the fuselage to the King Air. *Raytheon computer-generated photo*

RAYTHEON BEECHJET 400A
VITAL STATISTICS

Powerplants	Pratt & Whitney JT15D-5
Thrust per engine	2,900 lbs
Seats	7 to 8
Max. takeoff weight	16,100 lbs
Max. useful load	5,907 lbs
Max. cruise speed	Mach .78/450 kts
Range (45-minute reserves)	1,900 nm
FAA certified altitude	45,000 ft

Raytheon Premiere I

The Premiere I is Raytheon Aircraft's answer to Cessna's highly successful CitationJet. The 6 to 7 seat Premiere I (excluding cockpit seats) is certified for single-pilot operation. It is powered by two 2,300-pound thrust Williams-Rolls FJ44-2 engines, a more powerful version of the engines that powered the original CitationJet. Its maximum altitude is 45,000 feet; its cruise speed is Mach .80 at 41,000 feet, and its range is 1,500 nm with NBAA IFR reserves.

In the Raytheon tradition, the Premiere offers an exceptionally spacious cabin in comparison to its direct competitors without giving up any performance. Key to this accomplishment is a lightweight, carbon fiber/epoxy honeycomb fuselage mated to a metal swept wing. The Premier I is the first executive jet to make extensive use of composite construction technology. The lightweight fuselage employs the most modern composite construction techniques, using computer-controlled automated machines to weave the structure from individual carbon fiber threads over a composite honeycomb core. The result is a fuselage with similar strength to an equivalent metal fuselage and superior interior space.

This construction technique was developed by the company for the manufacture of the futuristic-looking composite Beechcraft Starship turboprop pusher canard. While pilots loved the Starship, it exceeded planned design weight (for reasons other than the composite construction) and didn't exceed the King Air's performance contrary to plans. Few were sold before production stopped, but the company perfected the composite construction technology that is being employed in the fuselage of the Premiere as well as the super midsized Hawker Horizon.

In the cockpit is the latest Collins Pro Line 21 avionics suite featuring a set of generous 8x10-inch LCD flat panel primary flight and multifunction displays (an additional display is an option). It is noteworthy that even the engine readings are displayed on the flat panel LCD MFD.

The Premiere is an intriguing twenty-first-century pure jet alternative to Raytheon's venerable King Air turboprop if no more than four to five passengers are to be carried. It is competitive both in terms of acquisition cost and operating costs and cleverly incorporates a faint hint of the King Air in its fuselage lines.

RAYTHEON PREMIERE I
VITAL STATISTICS

Powerplants	Williams-Rolls FJ44-2
Thrust per engine	2,300 lbs
Seats	6 to 7
Max. payload with full fuel	800 lbs
Max. cruise speed	Mach .80
Range (NBAA IFR reserves)	1,500 nm
Max. altitude	45,000 ft

Sino Swearingen SJ30

The Sino Swearingen SJ30 aims to be a player in the lightest end of the light-jet market, directly competing with the Cessna CitationJet and the Raytheon Premiere I. The SJ30 is designed by Ed Swearingen, the well-known, innovative aeronautical engineer, and made by Sino Swearingen, Inc., a joint venture between Sino Aerospace Investment Corporation and Swearingen Aircraft, Inc. It is designed for single-pilot operation and seats four to five in the cabin in addition to the two seats in the cockpit.

The SJ30 made its maiden flight in November 1996, equipped with the Williams-Rolls FJ44-1 engines that also power the CitationJet. The 1,900-pound thrust FJ44-1s were installed because the more powerful Dash 2 version of the engine for which the airplane was designed was not yet available. In September 1997 the SJ30 became the first airplane to fly with the 2,300-pound thrust FJ44-2.

The all-metal SJ30 is a sleek, elegant airplane in the Swearingen tradition. With its highly swept wings and tail, certification to 49,000 feet, and the low-cost, super efficient Williams-Rolls engine, it audaciously

The VisionAire Vantage is the lightest executive jet, powered by a single Pratt & Whitney JT15D-5 engine. It is aimed at owners/pilots not only of turboprops but even high-end piston airplanes, such as the Raytheon Bonanza and Piper Malibu Mirage. *VisionAire*

aspires to outdo its direct competitors in operating economy and performance. High-speed cruise is in excess of Mach .80. Its NBAA IFR range is 2,500 nm in long-range cruise at Mach .78 with four occupants (pilot and three passengers), giving it even transcontinental reach under some weather scenarios.

SINO SWEARINGEN SJ30
VITAL STATISTICS

Powerplants	Williams-Rolls FJ44-2
Thrust per engine	2,300 lbs
Seats	6 to 7 (including pilots)
Max. takeoff weight	13,200 lbs
Max. useful load	5,600 lbs
Normal cruise speed	Mach .80
Range (NBAA IFR reserves)	2,500 nm
Max. altitude	49,000 ft

VisionAire Vantage

The sleek, curvaceous VisionAire Vantage represents the most radical departure from convention in light executive jet design. It has a composite airframe. It has only one engine. Its acquisition price and operating costs are projected to be approximately 40 percent below the closest competing light twin jet, yet its performance will be only marginally less. The six-seat, single-pilot Vantage promises a range of 1,100 nm at a maximum cruise speed of 350 kts and a certified ceiling of 41,000 feet. In long-range cruise at 250 kts it is expected to have a reach of approximately 1,575 nm.

This lightest of executive jets is clearly taking aim at the turboprop market and even owners of high-end piston aircraft, encouraged by the growing acceptability of such single-engine turboprops as the TBM 700 and the Pilatus PC-12. To make the airplane a successful niche player, VisionAire founder, North Carolinian entrepreneur James O. Rice, is relying on his business savvy and the aviation experience of the Vantage team he assembled, which includes Burt Rutan—whose fingerprints are all over the carbon fiber airframe.

The Vantage's single engine is the proven Pratt & Whitney JT15D-5 engine that provides 2,965 pounds of thrust and powers the Citation Ultra and other executive jets. Lower acquisition and operating costs motivated the selection of the single, more powerful engine over the alternative of two lower thrust Williams-Rolls FJ44s.

An interesting feature of the airframe is the Vantage's forward swept wing, superficially reminiscent of the German Hansa Jet of the 1960s. The forward sweep is a clever technique to allow the wing spar to pass through the fuselage aft of the cabin, yet provide the desired center of gravity range. This arrangement is an elegantly simple way of eliminating a step that would be formed by the spar in the middle of the cabin floor if the wing were conventionally laid out. The alternative of retaining the conventional wing layout and eliminating the step with a complex carry-through design was deemed too costly.

Composite construction of the fuselage provides, as on the Raytheon Premiere I, a greater interior cabin space than is available in a metal fuselage of comparable external size. The cabin is sufficiently large to accommodate a flush lavatory, an option that is becoming practically obligatory in light jets.

The Vantage is a high risk start-up venture, but by mid-1998, when the project was in the production prototype stage, the company had already booked over 100 firm orders from a market hungry for innovation. Leading the marketing program was James B. Taylor, credited with launching the Falcon Jet, the Cessna Citation, and the Challenger. If that track record and the experience of the VisionAire technical team is anything to go by, the VisionAire Vantage may indeed be in the vanguard of a light jet revolution.

VISIONAIRE VANTAGE I VITAL STATISTICS

Powerplants	Pratt & Whitney JT15D-5
Thrust per engine	2,965 lbs
Seats (including pilot)	6
Max. takeoff weight	7,500 lbs
Max. useful load	3,200 lbs
Max. cruise speed	350 kts
Range (IFR reserves)	1,575 nm
Max altitude	41,000 ft

The Sino Swearingen SJ30-2 is another entrant into the Williams-Rolls FJ44-powered lightest end of the light-jet market. *Paul Bowen*

3

MIDSIZED JETS

Midsized executive jets currently in production generally have a range of 1,500 nm to 3,000 nm, a seating capacity of eight to nine passengers, and a price tag $10 to 15 million. They are also distinguished from all light jets with the exception of the Citation Excel by having a stand-up cabin that is an especially welcome comfort feature on long trips. Several of these aircraft are capable of nonstop transcontinental flights, though most of them are used for shorter distances which are more characteristic of the majority of business trips.

The Citation VII is a more powerful, glass cockpit-equipped version of the Citation III. It was Cessna's flagship jet until the appearance of the Citation X. *Cessna*

The Citation VII's glass cockpit features a Honeywell SPZ-8000 avionics suite that forms the foundation of more updated versions. *Cessna*

Among these airplanes is the world's fastest business jet, the Cessna Citation X which is capable of cruising at Mach .92. In 1996 the Citation X and its design team were awarded the prestigious Collier Trophy by the National Aeronautics Administration for outstanding design.

A new trend in the development of this group of aircraft is to design them with range and comfort that approaches the capabilities of the large executive jets but at a midsized price. New construction technology including the use of composites, advanced wing designs, and more efficient engines are enabling designers to push the performance envelope of these "super midsized" aircraft to new levels. The first among them is the Galaxy Aerospace Galaxy featuring an exceptionally wide cabin and nonstop Paris–New York range. Following the Galaxy is Raytheon's Hawker Horizon, the descendant of the most stately of midsized jets, the Hawker 800, and its predecessors.

Bombardier Learjet 60

The Learjet 60 pulled off somewhat of a coup when it was introduced in 1995. While it retained the traditional Learjet performance that has made the company's aircraft the executive jet equivalent of the sexiest sports car, its stand-up six- to eight-seat passenger cabin laid to rest the perception that Learjet performance comes at the expense of passenger comfort.

The Learjet 60 is derived from the company's first midsized jet, the Learjet 55, but it is a substantially different airplane. It is equipped with two Pratt & Whitney Canada PW305A turbofans, flat rated to 4,600 pounds at sea level; they are considerably more powerful as well as more fuel efficient than the Learjet 55's Garrett 731.

The new engines required considerable redesign of the fuselage aerodynamics. Learjet also made significant aerodynamic improvements in the winglets' performance. NASA's TRANAIR airflow modeling computer program was used extensively in the Learjet 60's aerodynamic development. Other major changes were a stretched fuselage to improve cabin comfort, and make possible the full-cabin-width lavatory and the installation of a Collins Proline avionics suite in the cockpit.

The Mach .92 Cessna Citation X is the world's fastest business jet. Its highly swept, supercritical wing and streamlined fuselage push the limits of aerodynamic design. The Citation X's design team won the prestigious Collier Trophy for their efforts. *Cessna*

A lot of time also went into engineering the Lear-jet 60's cockpit ergonomics, and the effort has paid off. Everything is within effortless fingertip reach. Most systems' controls and switches run across the bottom of the instrument panel and are neatly boxed per system.

The Learjet 60 was among one of the first airplanes of its size to be equipped with FADEC, which stands for "full authority digital engine controls." That means control by wire. There are no mechanical linkages between the cockpit and the engines. It is all done by software. Pioneered in airline use, FADEC is fed all the information it needs from the airplane's other systems and sensors and automatically sets the required power.

With FADEC has come an even higher degree of cockpit automation. Engine start is literally a single push of a button per engine. There are five power settings for the thrust levers: engine cut-off, idle, maxi-

mum cruise power, maximum continuous power, take-off, and automatic performance reserve. In case of an engine failure FADEC even increases power by one-third on the remaining engine.

FADEC's redundancy makes it as safe if not safer than traditional mechanical linkages. There are two totally independent control units, each hooked up to different sensors. The system also has its own separate alternator to power the engine electronics. On start-up the system goes through a self diagnosis, comparing the two units (channels). If there are any discrepancies the engines simply won't start. If all is well, the system automatically selects one channel and maintains the other one on standby. To make equal use of both channels, the standby channel is selected as the primary channel during the next engine cycle. The crew can also manually select a channel of preference.

The Citation X's cockpit is equipped with a Honeywell Primus 2000 avionics suite, including EICAS. *Cessna*

The panel is equipped with a Collins Pro Line 4 avionics suite. There are four integrated displays. Each pilot has a primary flight display (PFD) and a multi-function display (MFD). The PFD contains in one single display all the flight and navigation information that pilots previously had to acquire through their traditional instrument scan from a handful of separate instruments. Dual air data computers and attitude heading reference systems provide flight data to the displays and the autopilot/flight director. Among the capabilities of the MFD are the display of moving maps, color radar, checklists, and diagnostic messages.

At its maximum takeoff weight of 23,500 pounds the Learjet 60 can climb directly to 43,000 feet in standard conditions. Its optimum operating altitudes are in the high 40s, well above most airline traffic, and it is certified all the way up to FL 510.

The secret to the Learjet 60's excellent climb performance lies in large measure in its powerful Pratt & Whitney Canada PW305A engines. While they are flat rated to 4,600 pounds of thrust each at sea level, they are certified to putting out 5,225 pounds. As the aircraft climbs, this reserve power provides a degree of compensation for the diminishing engine performance in the increasingly rarefied atmosphere.

In the air the Learjet 60 handles like a pussycat, much in the tradition of the lighter Learjet 31A. Like the 31A, it is equipped with aft delta fins which continue generating lift when the wing stalls, thus pitching the nose down to recover from the stall. For this reason the 60 has only a stick shaker as a stall warning device. As on the 31A, the delta fins eliminate the need for a stick pusher.

The efficient Pratt & Whitneys, the high aspect ratio wing, and the airframe's refined aerodynamics, coupled with a hefty useful load of 9,110 pounds, give the Learjet 60 transcontinental range with a full cabin. The maximum usable fuel load of 7,910 pounds leaves room for 1,200 pounds of payload, enough to accommodate six average-sized passengers and their luggage and carry them 2,325 nm with 45-minute fuel reserves. And on the shorter stage lengths of the typical executive flight, even the most well-fed line-up of movers and shakers and all their golf gear would have a hard time busting the airplane's weight and balance limits.

BOMBARDIER LEARJET 60 VITAL STATISTICS

Powerplants	Pratt & Whitney PW305A
Thrust per engine	4,600 lbs
Seats	8 to 9
Max. takeoff weight	23,500 lbs
Max. useful load	9,110 lbs
Max. Mach operating speed	Mach .81
Range (45-min reserves)	2,325 nm
FAA certified altitude	51,000 ft

Cessna Citation VII

In 1998 the Citation VII continued in production as one of Cessna's two midsized jets, a smaller stablemate of the exotic Citation X. Its roots go back to 1990 when the company announced the imminent replacement of the Citation III by two derivative aircraft. One

Facing page

There isn't a straight line on the Citation X's advanced airframe. The powerful Allison-Rolls AE3007C engines aren't as large as the huge air intake, necessitated by airflow considerations, suggests. *Cessna*

was the no-frills Citation VI. The other was the more expensive Citation VII which benefited from a power upgrade to improve its performance, and a glass avionics suite to update its cockpit. It received its airworthiness certificate in January 1992.

The Citation VII is a graceful aircraft equipped with the same advanced technology swept wings as the Citation III. Its most significant advance over the Citation III was an increase of 430 pounds in thrust per engine, delivered by the 4,080-pound thrust Garrett TFE 731-4R that replaced the earlier 3B versions. With this increase in engine power, the Citation VII can climb directly to 43,000 feet at maximum takeoff weight, and in the final stages of a flight, with most of its fuel burned off, it is light enough to reach its certified altitude of 51,000 feet.

The objective of the upgrade, successfully accomplished, was to improve hot and high performance. The thrust increase only amounted to approximately 12 percent, but it greatly expanded the airplane's operational flexibility in hot and high conditions, permitting it to carry more fuel and payload under these circumstances. For example, the Citation VII can takeoff from mile-high Denver on a 90-degree day with four passengers and fly over 2,000 nm with NBAA IFR reserves. This figure is close to its 2,220-nm range in high cruise at 476 knots. It is also a feat the Citation III would fall well short of without refueling en route. Upping the Citation VII's thrust was a strategic move similar to Raytheon's upgrade of the Hawker 800 to the 800XP later in the decade.

The cockpit is equipped with the Honeywell SPZ-8000 avionics suite that includes four standard (and a fifth optional) EFIS displays. There is greater integration of information on the more recent PFDs and MFDs, but, nevertheless, the SPZ-8000 is a pilot's delight.

The Citation VII's stand-up cabin seats six to eight, and Cessna has put great emphasis on its interior finish, given its fleet flagship status until the arrival of the Citation X. Customers have many interior finish options and can easily achieve a rich understated elegance that ranks up there with the best quality the largest executive jet cabins have to offer. There is also a spacious, full-cabin-width aft lavatory. A drawback to the cabin is a step in the aisle just before the lavatory, where the wing spar passes through the fuselage. This somewhat inconvenient feature is absent in the straight-wing Excel which otherwise has an identical cabin.

Owning the fastest business jet in the world doesn't mean that you have to skimp on interior space and comfort. The Citation X's cabin configured for eight. *Cessna*

CITATION VII VITAL STATISTICS

Powerplants	Garrett TFE 731-4R
Thrust per engine	4,080 lbs
Seats	6 to 8
Max. takeoff weight	22,450 lbs
Max. useful load	10,880 lbs
Max. Mach operating speed	.83
Range (45-min reserves)	2,220 nm
FAA certified altitude	51,000 ft

Cessna Citation X

As discussed earlier, Cessna achieved one of the biggest marketing coups with the Citation line by creating a pure jet that was tame enough to enable pilots moving up from turboprop equipment to make an easy

Key to the Astra SPX's high performance is its double-swept, supercritical wing, which features leading edge slats in addition to trailing edge Fowler flaps. *Galaxy Aerospace*

transition. The characteristics that made it a success, however, also gave its detractors ammunition for criticism. The straight-winged Citations were considerably slower than other executive jets, leading wags to give them such derisive nicknames as Nearjet and Slowtation.

The line's slowpoke reputation improved with the introduction of the swept-wing midsized Citations, starting with the Citation III, but it was the Mach .92 Citation X, the fastest business jet in the world, that decisively put to rest all quips about a lack of speed.

A superficial glance at the Citation X suggests that its high speed is due to its two enormous Allison-Rolls engines that seem to be way out of scale with the rest of the airplane. The engines, however, are only part of the story. Equally important is its sophisticated low drag airframe.

Simply hanging ever bigger engines on an existing executive jet to make it go faster is not a good solution beyond a certain point because it ceases to be economical, and the airframe will encounter aerodynamic limits that no amount of power can overcome. To maximize speed, an airframe that pushes the limits of aerodynamic design is also necessary in addition to optimally bigger engines.

Cessna's engineers spent countless hours performing Computational Fluid Dynamics analyses to establish the Citation X's airframe design and applied various drag reduction techniques. The most obvious is the radical sweep of the wing and tail surfaces. The wing is swept back 37 degrees, more than the wing of any other business jet. The vertical and horizontal stabilizer are also highly swept.

Wing sweep delays the speed at which a wing encounters the onset of compressibility and the associated dramatic increase in drag as the airflow reaches supersonic speed (also referred to as Critical Mach speed). Airflow accelerates at different rates over the various curved surfaces of an airframe. Close to the speed of sound, airflow over certain areas of the wing (and, to a lesser degree, the fuselage) can accelerate to the speed of sound locally while the entire airplane is still flying considerably below the speed of sound. As Mach 1 is approached in this local area, a supersonic shock wave begins to form. Drag greatly increases, and the shock wave may separate, which can cause control problems and limits the maximum Mach operating speed of a subsonic airplane.

Airflow acceleration is most rapid over the most curved section of an airfoil. The greater the difference in rates of curvature of a section of a wing surface, the greater the difference in airflow acceleration over the different areas. To achieve a more uniform airflow acceleration over a straight wing, two options are available. The airfoil can be made as thin and as gradually curved as possible. It can also be swept. When the wing is swept, the airflow, which continues to flow parallel to the fuselage, traverses a longer distance over the swept wing's surface along a more gradually curved profile, resulting in less difference in rates of local area acceleration. The greater the sweep of the wing, the more uniform the rate of airflow acceleration, and the higher the speed of the aircraft at which any local area of the wing reaches Critical Mach.

The downside of a highly swept wing is its handling at low speed and high angles of attack, when the airflow has a tendency to be diverted outward along the wing and separate erratically from the wing surface causing unstable stall characteristics. Wing fences and vortilons that shepherd the airflow along the desired path at low speeds are the traditional solution on airplanes that want to avoid complex high lift devices, but Cessna opted for the latter option. Outboard slats that deploy automatically at a certain angle of attack and with the extension of the flaps, maintain high lift at low speeds allowing a healthy airflow over the ailerons and ensuring low takeoff and landing speeds.

Local area airflow can also go critical on the fuselage of an aircraft operating near the speed of sound. Particularly vulnerable local areas are sharply curved sections such as the wing fuselage junction and the engine pylons. Keeping airflow acceleration over the fuselage is the reason for the large elongated underside of the Citation X that minimizes the rate of curvature and resembles an equipment pod found on some military aircraft that carry a lot of ECM gear or other specialized equipment.

The Galaxy Aerospace Galaxy is the first of the super mid-sized jets with a wide cabin. Nonstop Paris–New York range and highly competitive acquisition and operating costs make the Galaxy an attractive proposition. Here the aircraft is on its second flight. *Galaxy Aerospace*

The Citation X design team's aerodynamic efforts paid off handsomely. The airplane has been test flown all the way to Mach .98, only 2 percent below the speed of sound, with no ill effects, and it can easily achieve its maximum Mach operating limit of .92 in cruise.

To propel its artwork of an airframe at the speeds for which it was designed, Cessna selected high bypass Allison-Rolls AE3007C turbofans for which it was the launch customer. The engines are flat rated for the Citation X to 6,400 pounds of thrust each but are capable of 7,200 pounds, providing low wear and tear and room to expand. The Allisons are operated by FADEC, taking all the mystery out of power management.

The cabin is competitively comfortable in the midsized class, except compared to the new Galaxy's interior. Normal configuration is for 8 passengers in a double club configuration, though a layout for 12 is also available. In the cockpit the Honeywell Primus 2000 avionics package provides state-of-the-art flight management. The five large 7x8-inch display screens include an EICAS display.

The Citation X is certified to 51,000 feet and can climb directly to 43,000 feet at maximum takeoff weight. It has a range of 2,600 nm in high cruise of Mach .90 and 3,000 nm in long-range cruise of Mach .85 with NBAA IFR reserves. While its engines consume more fuel per hour at equivalent power settings than competing aircraft, the Citation X is faster in long-range cruise than its closest competitor in high-speed cruise and will burn less fuel in long-range cruise than the competition in high-speed cruise. So it is not only the airplane to buy to go fast but also the preferred choice to go fast economically—a worthy winner of the Collier Trophy.

CITATION X VITAL STATISTICS

Powerplants	Allison-Rolls AE3007C
Thrust per engine	6,400 lbs
Seats (excluding pilots)	8 to 12
Max. takeoff weight	35,700 lbs
Max. useful load	16,624 lbs
Max. Mach operating speed	.92
Range (45-min reserves)	3,250 nm
FAA certified altitude	51,000 ft

Galaxy Aerospace Astra SPX

The Israeli Air Force's proudest tradition is its formidable ability to maintain air superiority. In introducing the Astra SPX, the latest version of the Astra business jet, Israel Aircraft Industries may well have succeeded in transferring some of that tradition to the executive jet performance wars. The Astra SPX is among the fastest and longest range jets in its class.

The six- to nine-seat Astra SPX weighs in at a maximum takeoff weight of 24,650 pounds. It is a refined and considerably upgraded version of the Astra SP that was certified in 1986 and established the line's solid reputation for high performance. Although produced by Israel Aircraft Industries, the Astra has its roots in the United States. The lineage goes all the way back to the Rockwell Commander, a competitor to the original Learjet. Israel Aircraft Industries bought Rockwell's executive jet line in the 1970s and produced the IAI Westwind light jet, a direct descendant of the Rockwell Commander until 1986 when it introduced the larger Astra, a completely new design of its own.

The challenge in aircraft design is to strike just the right balance between competing characteristics to optimize performance. For a given set of performance goals the lightest, aerodynamically-cleanest possible airframe coupled with the most powerful yet most fuel efficient engines is the holy grail. The relationship between these factors determines how far an aircraft will be able to carry a given load of passengers and their baggage and how fast it will get them there; in other words, it determines how competitive it will be.

Everyone has access to the same engines, so a lot rides on the airframe design. Complicating the challenge are the twin demands of being able to cruise near the speed of sound and takeoff and land at speeds low enough to have the flexibility of using the shortest available airfields. And it all has to be done for a price tag that makes the private jet sound economic proposition.

IAI saw the Astra's competitive opportunity in a high performance complex wing with features that are usually found only on larger transport category jets. The sleek, thin, double-swept wing developed for the Astra SP is ideal for high-speed flight. The winglets, introduced on the SPX, reduce drag around the wingtips, further enhancing high-speed efficiency.

But such a slippery wing stops generating lift at a relatively high airspeed, which would result in fast approach speeds and would put many short runways off limits. To perform well at low speed, the wing has to be able to change its contour. The solution is to design a wing that can significantly increase its curvature (camber). The more cambered the wing's surface, the more lift it will generate, and the lower its stall speed will be.

Flaps alone would not have yielded the desired low-speed performance for the Astra's highly swept wing, so IAI opted for leading edge slats that deploy simultaneously with the flaps. Slats are a common feature on major airliners but are found only on the Astra, its larger stablemate, the Galaxy, and the Citation X among midsized executive jets in production.

The complex wing design has achieved its low-speed performance objective. At maximum takeoff weight the SPX needs only 5,235 feet of runway (at sea level in standard atmospheric conditions), and at maximum landing weight its runway requirement is only 2,720 feet. At the lighter weights that are typical of trips in the 300–700-nm range, the SPX can comfortably operate out of 3,000 airstrips with a full passenger load under a wide variety of conditions.

To keep the airframe's weight in check, IAI used composites extensively throughout the airframe. Almost the entire nose (which lifts up like the bonnet of an E-Type Jaguar to reveal the avionics bay), the gear doors, the baggage doors, the oxygen tanks, and the tips of the tail surfaces are composite, and the ailerons are a honeycomb nomex structure.

Having gotten the most out of the Astra SP's airframe, IAI upped the competitive ante on the SPX by giving it more powerful engines, AlliedSignal TFE 731-40s. They are one of the latest versions of that workhorse of executive jet engines, producing 4,250 pounds of thrust each, compared to 3,700 pounds per side provided by the Garrett 731-3As on the Astra SP. Improved fuel specifics and the ability to get to fuel efficient altitudes faster make the Dash 40s more miserly fuel consumers than the Dash 3As in spite of the increased power.

The SPX can carry four passengers and their luggage 3,025 nm at an economy cruise of Mach .75 with NBAA IFR reserves, climbing directly to 41,000 feet and reaching its maximum operating altitude of 45,000 feet within the hour. At maximum cruise of Mach .82 the range with the same payload is 2,500 nm with NBAA IFR reserves.

To manage all this performance, IAI has given the SPX a pilot's cockpit equipped with a state-of-the-art Collins Pro Line 4 avionics suite including dual primary flight displays (PFD), multifunction displays (MFD), and a GNS-X global navigation system.

Power is managed by the Astra's digital electronic engine control (DEEC). DEEC handles the entire start sequence and automatically-set takeoff power, allowing the pilot to simply firewall the thrust levers on takeoff. DEEC differs from full authority digital engine control (FADEC) only in the sense that it doesn't have automatic climb and cruise settings.

Another interesting feature of the Astra is its passenger cabin. Its oval shape provides the most efficient way of maximizing useful interior space while minimizing the fuselage cross-section so important for keeping down drag. While the cabin width is on the narrow

A strong suit of the Galaxy, in addition to its long-range for a midsized price, is its wide, sumptuous cabin that rivals the cabins of larger, more expensive jets. *Galaxy Aerospace*

Following pages
The Hawker 800XP is the most refined version of the most stately midsized executive jets and traces its lineage back to the industry's beginnings. *Raytheon*

A fine view of the Hawker 800XP. It is not widely realized that this airplane can operate off rough dirt and grass strips. *Raytheon*

side for midsized jets, the sides of the fuselage are nearly vertical, allowing for comfortable headroom and shoulder room for seated passengers. A dropped, full-cabin-length aisle provides sufficient vertical space to put the Astra in the stand-up cabin league.

ASTRA SPX VITAL STATISTICS

Powerplants	AlliedSignal TFE 731-40
Thrust per engine	4,250 lbs
Seats	6 to 9
Max. takeoff weight	24,650 lbs
Max. useful load	11,100 lbs
Max. Mach operating speed	.87
Range (NBAA IFR reserves)	3,025 nm
FAA certified altitude	45,000 ft

Galaxy Aerospace Galaxy

The Astra SPX proved to be an executive jet of exceptional performance in the midsize class, making it particularly challenging for the company to come up with a complementary airplane to broaden the product line. An innovative design philosophy, however, that set high mission objectives yielded an airplane eminently worthy of being the Astra's stablemate. It is the Galaxy, the first of the super midsize jets which was designed to provide large executive jet performance and cabin comfort at a midsize price and operating costs.

This ambitious goal was achieved by relying on an advanced version of the Astra's proven high performance double swept-wing design mated to a widebody fuselage propelled by two highly efficient Pratt &

Whitney 306A engines that deliver 5,700 pounds of thrust each. The disciplined emphasis on getting the most performance out of what the designers had to work with delivered impressive results.

The Galaxy's maximum range of 3,698 nm is approximately 20 percent in excess of its nearest midsize competitors and only 14 percent under the reach of the Gulfstream IV-SP. It can get in and out of considerably shorter fields than its larger rivals. Its operating costs are significantly less over trips of similar length, yet its widebody cabin approaches the comfort of the large executive jets. A good benchmark of its capabilities is that it can fly the 3,650 nm between New York and Paris nonstop with four passengers and NBAA IFR reserves at Mach .75 at a lower operating cost than any other executive jet that can do the trip. At Mach .80 its reach is 3,200 nm with NBAA IFR reserves carrying eight passengers.

The Galaxy's cockpit is state of the art, equipped with a five-tube Collins Pro Line 4 avionics suite. Two sets of screens consist of a primary flight display and multifunction display each. The fifth screen is an engine information and crew alerting system (EICAS) that intelligently displays information on an as needed basis. This display method is also known as the dark cockpit approach, a reference to an automatic absence of displayed information unless it is relevant. Navigation is provided by a UNS-1C integrated flight management system. The Galaxy also features dual digital radio display and control panels positioned at the pilot's eye level that becomes the standby HSI display if need be.

From an owner's perspective one of the Galaxy's strongest attributes is its widebody cockpit. It is the only midsize jet wide enough to feature a four-place dining/conference area with the aisle and a buffet set off to one side. For comfortable night flying the dining area seats convert into a double bed. In front of this area in typical configuration are four seats in a club seating arrangement. The stand-up cabin's height is a generous 6 feet, 3 inches.

The Galaxy made its maiden flight in December 1997 from Israel Aircraft Industries' facilities at Ben Gurion Airport, followed by a certification program lasting into 1998. Given the Galaxy's attributes (that are more in line with the large executive jets than its

midsize competitors) combined with its midsize cost and operating economy, it should prove a formidable competitor in coming years.

GALAXY VITAL STATISTICS

Powerplants	Pratt & Whitney 306A
Thrust per engine	5,700 lbs
Seats	8-10
Normal takeoff weight	33,450 lbs
Max. useful load	15,200 lbs
Cruise speed	Mach .80
Range (NBAA IFR reserves)	3,698 nm
Max. altitude	45,000 ft

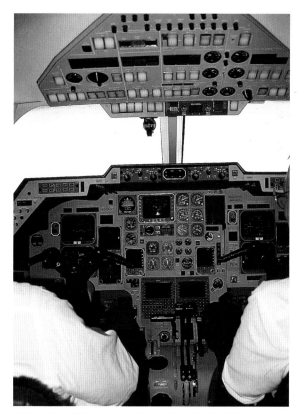

A Hawker 800 en route from Little Rock, Arkansas, to Boston, Massachusetts. Note the Concorde-like control columns. Many pilots find them more pleasant and natural to operate than the traditional yokes. *Geza Szurouy*

Hawker 800XP

The Hawker 800XP is Raytheon's top of the line executive jet, fitting in between the smaller Beechjet and Premiere, and the super midsized Horizon (debuting in 1999). The Hawker traces its roots back to the HS 125 series of executive jets initiated by deHavilland, which became a division of Hawker Siddeley by the time the prototype was developed. The two firms were among the greatest of Britain's aircraft makers of the past, known for such creations as the deHavilland Mosquito and the Hawker Hurricane of Battle of Britain fame.

Until 1993 the Hawker 800 and its now discontinued larger derivative, the 1000, formed the business jet line of British Aerospace. But while the Hawkers benefited greatly from British Aerospace's expertise gained on such projects as the Airbus and the support of the Concorde, increasingly they were not the best strategic fit with the company's much bigger defense and airline businesses.

At the same time on the other side of the Atlantic, Raytheon was facing a strategic challenge of a different sort. It had the turboprop market cornered with the prestigious King Air line, but it had only one light executive jet, the Beechjet. It was looking to expand the jet product line, and the Hawkers were an excellent fit. A deal was struck with British Aerospace, and the acquisition of the Hawker line made Raytheon a major player in the highly competitive business jet market. Manufacturing initially continued in England with final completion in the United States, but in 1996 the entire Hawker production line was moved to Wichita.

The Hawker 800XP is an upgraded replacement version of the 800, introduced in 1996. The main difference between the Hawker 800 and 800XP is the XP's upgraded version of the 800's AlliedSignal TFE 731-5 engine which increases thrust per side by 360 pounds to 4,660 pounds. The more powerful engines permit a 500-pound increase in useful load, but more importantly the extra power significantly improves the airplane's short field performance and its performance at high altitude airports in hot and humid conditions. Aerodynamic drag has also been reduced with the replacement of the stall fences on the wing with the much smaller but equally effective vortilons.

The demands of intensive international operations were also a prime consideration in the Hawker's development. The cockpit is among the roomiest in its class, and its layout also has the feel of an airliner's flight deck. An unusual feature is the motorcycle-style handlebar on each control column, instead of the more conventional yoke, similar to the control column of the Concorde.

The Hawker 800XP is available with Honeywell or Collins avionics systems. The well organized panel equipped with either package includes dual attitude heading reference systems, dual air data computer systems, and a five-tube EFIS display that has become an industry standard. Dual UNS 1-B navigation systems are within easy reach just ahead of the thrust levers. While the engines do not have a full FADEC system (full authority digital engine control, which operates the engines electronically by wire instead of mechanical linkages), it is equipped with DEEC that allows the pilot to move the thrust levers full forward and rely on the fuel computer to automatically set the appropriate N^1 power (fan speed).

In addition, the Hawker has an interesting feature found on several executive jets to assist the pilot in case of an engine failure. An automatic power reserve kicks in on the good engine, and a rudder bias system assists in compensating for the yaw caused by the asymmetric thrust.

The Hawker 800XP is certified to 41,000 feet in the United States and 43,000 feet in the United Kingdom (the difference is due to a minor variance in certification standards). It is a big airplane for a midsized jet, weighing in at a maximum takeoff weight of 28,000 pounds with a hefty maximum fuel capacity of 10,000 pounds and a maximum payload (passengers and baggage) of 2,000 pounds.

The long and the short of the numbers is that the airplane can fly a standard load of eight passengers and their baggage over 2,400 nm with IFR reserves. That means it can fly nonstop anywhere within the lower 48 states in the United States or anywhere within Europe. It also makes possible such nonstop flights as New York–Mexico City, Beijing–New Delhi, and Caracas–Sao Paulo. The Hawker 800/800XP has enjoyed worldwide popularity with over 300 in service. Several oil companies even operate them from unimproved gravel strips.

The Hawker Horizon (foreground) is an all-new design in the tradition of the Hawker line. It offers longer range and 60 percent more cabin space than the 800XP. Here it "flies" in formation with the Premiere I in a computer-generated image. *Raytheon*

In many ways the popular 800XP looks more like a mini-airliner than a midsized business jet. Its stately lines and promise of lavish comfort are reminders that the Hawkers were designed as much for government VIP use as for corporate flight departments. Raytheon operates a completion center in Little Rock, Arkansas (as does Dassault for its Falcons), to create the luxurious environment executives have come to expect from these jets. The styling center does the paint, interior, and avionics installations for the Hawker line. A big selling point of the airplanes is that every Hawker has a custom interior.

The center maintains a network of over 500 suppliers of exotic woods, leather, ultrasuede, silk, and other items. Some of the material used is quite extraordinary, even by the exacting weight control standards of aviation. The nomex honeycomb cabin wall panels, for example, can withstand a 9-g collision with a 100-pound bag yet are so light that they can be easily lifted with two fingers.

In the midsized class the Hawker's cabin is among the most spacious and comfortable. There is stand-up headroom along its entire length with no spars lurking around on the floor to trip passengers when they least expect it. The most popular layout is a club arrangement in the front part of the cabin and a three-person sofa across from another seat aft. All the seats swivel 360 degrees. Turning the aft seat to face the sofa creates an area quite independent of the forward club seats, giving passengers a great deal of flexibility in working and socializing. The sofa can also be converted into a comfortable bed. There is a full-cabin-width bathroom in the back with access to the items stowed in the rear baggage compartment, which can be convenient for a pre-arrival change of clothing on long trips. There is also another large baggage compartment up front between the cabin and the cockpit.

HAWKER 800XP VITAL STATISTICS

Powerplants	AlliedSignal TFE 731-5BR
Thrust per engine	4,660 lbs
Seats	8 to 12
Max. takeoff weight	28,000 lbs
Max. useful load	12,020 lbs
Cruise speed (typical)	443 kts
Range (IFR reserves)	2,432 nm
FAA certified altitude	41,000 ft

Hawker Horizon

At the 1996 NBAA convention Raytheon Aircraft introduced its new entry into the super midsize business jet market, the Hawker Horizon, with the first flight planned for late 1999. Inspired by the successful Hawker line and the company's

experience with composite construction technology gained on the turboprop Starship program, the Horizon promises to be Raytheon's twenty-first-century jet.

According to initial specifications, the Horizon's range is 3,400 nm; its maximum cruise speed is Mach .84, and the volume of its stand-up cabin is 60 percent greater than the cabin of the Hawker 800XP. Its construction is mixed, similar to the Premiere light jet, with a carbon fiber/epoxy honeycomb fuselage and metal wings. The cabin features a flat floor (no trench walkway in the center with raised seats on the two sides) which provides generous legroom for seated passengers. Center club and double club seating for eight are among the configuration options. The aft baggage compartment is accessible from both the sizable lavatory and from the outside.

The wing has a supercritical airfoil and a 30-degree sweep. It is optimized for high-speed performance and low-speed handling characteristics. It is made for Raytheon by Fuji Heavy Industries of Japan, the company that also manufactures the center section for the Boeing 777.

Power is provided by two Pratt & Whitney PW308A engines developed specifically for the Horizon. The engines produce 6,500 pounds of thrust each and are controlled by FADEC. The cockpit features a Honeywell Primus Epic avionics suite. The five large LCD flat-panel displays which are becoming a cockpit layout standard in the industry include a central engine information and crew alert system (EICAS) display.

HAWKER HORIZON VITAL STATISTICS

Powerplants	Pratt & Whitney 308A
Thrust per engine	6,500 lbs
Seats	8-10
Payload with full fuel	3,570 lbs
Max. Mach operating speed	Mach .84
Range (45-min reserves)	3,400 nm
Max. altitude	45,000 ft

4

HEAVY HAULERS

Large executive jets carry the greatest number of passengers the longest distances among business aircraft. They generally have the capacity to carry 10 to 12 passengers in normal configuration and more if they have optional higher density seating. Their range is generally between 3,000 nm and 4,500 nm, which gives all of them U.S. transcontinental capability and several of them trans-Atlantic reach under a variety of loading and wind conditions. Their price range (as of 1998) is from $17 to $35 million.

The Challenger 604 whisking its passengers out of San Francisco. Bombardier

There are three manufacturers producing large business jets. Dassault of France makes the Falcon series, Bombardier of Canada the Challenger 604, and Gulfstream of the United States the G-IV SP. In addition, Bombardier makes a Special Edition version of its Regional Jet airliner for corporate use by replacing the airline interior with a corporate interior.

The market is relatively mature for large executive jets, and all of the current production aircraft are at or close to the limits of available technology. New designs are unlikely to appear in this category for some time to come because they can't deliver a sufficiently greater level of performance, economy, and comfort compared to current production models to justify the development cost.

Bombardier Challenger 604

The widebody Challenger 604, introduced into service in 1996, is a development of the Challenger 601. It combines the 601 airframe with a more powerful powerplant and the up-to-date avionics and robust

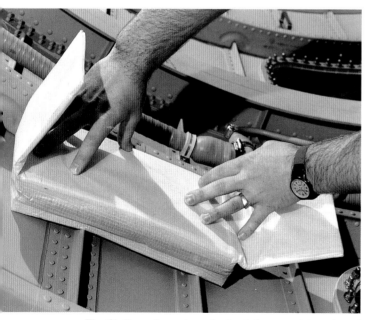

The Challenger's passive noise insulation material consists of one layer of fiberglass inserted between two layers of Polymide polymer foam. *Bombardier*

landing gear of the Regional Jet airliner, which itself is a derivative of the Challenger 600/601.

The Challenger is among the most popular large executive jets because of its extra-wide cabin. The cabin, which is wider but slightly shorter than competing cabins, is the most successful in conveying to passengers the sense of being in a normal room instead of a fuselage trying to camouflage itself. For many buyers of a large executive jets the cabin has been the swing factor in favor of the Challenger.

In terms of range, earlier models of the Challengers fell somewhat short of the longest legged Falcons and the Gulfstream IV-SP. The Challenger 601 had an IFR reach of 3,600 nm compared to 4,000 nm of the Falcon 900B, 4,200 nm for the G-IV SP, and 4,500 nm for the more recent Falcon 900EX. For many buyers this was not a big issue because the length of most business flights, even by the large jets, falls far short of maximum range—a strong incentive to opt for the most comfortable cabin. Nevertheless, the Challenger was losing some sales to operators with long-range needs, a drawback that is addressed by the Challenger 604.

Key to extending the Challenger's range was equipping the airplane with an updated version of the General Electric CF34 engines. They deliver 8,729 pounds of thrust each, which represents a 7-percent improvement over the earlier model that powers the last version of the Challenger 601, yet they are also more fuel efficient. Along with an increase in fuel load, they give the 604 an NBAA IFR range with five passengers and three crew onboard of 4,000 nm at a long-range cruise speed of Mach .74, which is a 400 nm increase over the 601 and takes all worries about fuel out of crossing the Atlantic westbound against prevailing winds. If speed is of the essence, at its normal cruise speed of Mach .80 the 604's reach is still a very respectable 3,700 nm.

To handle a 2,500-pound increase in maximum gross weight to 47,600 pounds and an increase in maximum landing weight by 2,000 pounds, the Challenger received the Regional Jet's rugged trailing link landing gear and brake system.

The Challenger 604's cockpit is a pilot's delight, equipped with the Collins Pro Line 4 avionics suite that had proved its mettle in the Regional Jet. Six flat-

The Challenger 604's Collins Pro Line 4 six-tube avionics suite. *Bombardier*

screen displays dominate, including two EICAS displays. Flight management is accomplished with a very capable Collins AVSAT 6000 FMS.

In the Challenger 604, Bombardier managed to marginalize the competition's advantages over earlier Challengers concerning the limits of range, enhance the airplane's strengths on flights of typical duration, and provide all this at a substantially lower price tag than any alternative. That is a combination that will make the Challenger one of the most popular large executive jets for years to come.

CHALLENGER 604 VITAL STATISTICS

Powerplants (2)	General Electric CF34-3B
Thrust per engine	8,729 lbs
Passengers (typical)	9 to 12
Max. takeoff weight	47,600 lbs
Max. useful load	21,070 lbs
Max. Mach operating speed	.85
Range (NBAA, IFR, 5 pax)	4,000 nm
FAA certified altitude	41,000 ft

Falcon 50EX

The sign of a good airplane is that with occasional, relatively minor upgrading it remains in production for decades. By that measure, the three-engined Falcon 50 has to be one of the most successful business airplanes ever, into its third decade of production. Dassault Aviation established a standard of its own with the original Falcon 50 when the airplane made its first flight in 1976. Three-engine redundancy and an advanced, supercritical double-swept wing with airline-style leading edge slats in addition to the massive trailing edge Fowler flaps gave the Falcon 50 a long reach and excellent short field and hot and high performance. Dubbed the "mini-727," it earned the affection of CEOs worldwide.

After a production run of almost two decades the Falcon 50 remained so popular that instead of phasing it out, Dassault decided to upgrade it with a new glass cockpit and new engines that produce more thrust at altitude. The objective was not only to increase the 50's range, but to enable the upgraded airplane to fly even its longest missions at a higher cruise speed.

The result was the Falcon 50EX. Its AlliedSignal TFE731-40s have the same maximum sea-level thrust as the original Falcon 50's TFE 731-3s, but at 40,000 feet at Mach .80 they crank out 24 percent more thrust and consume 7 percent less fuel. They also allow the EX to climb to 41,000 feet at maximum takeoff weight in 23 minutes, compared to the original 50's ability to reach 39,000 feet in 30 minutes.

As a result of this improved engine performance, in long-range cruise at Mach .75 the EX can carry eight passengers 3,265 nm with NBAA IFR reserves, an increase of 200 nm over the range of the original 50. Better still is the performance increase in high-speed cruise of Mach .80, which gives the EX a reach of 3,025 nm, a gain of 400 nm over its predecessor at the same speed. Another way of looking at it is that the Falcon 50EX can fly at Mach .80 as far as the original 50 could fly at Mach .75.

Equally impressive is the EX's hot and high performance. It can take off from Mexico City, where field elevation is 8,448 feet, on a 91-degree day with eight passengers and fly them 2,700 nm with NBAA IFR reserves.

In the cockpit the 50EX received the same Collins Pro Line 4 avionics as is installed in the Falcon 2000, which features two PFD displays and two MFD displays. Engine and systems information is displayed on three Sextant Avionique color LCD displays.

With its upgrade and highly competitive purchase price, the 50EX continues to serve a market that thinks three engines are better than two and is attracted by great value for a comparatively low investment.

FALCON 50EX VITAL STATISTICS

Powerplants (3)	AlliedSignal TFE731-40
Thrust per engine	3,700 lbs
Passengers (typical)	10 to 12
Max. takeoff weight	39,700 lbs
Max. useful load	17,000 lbs
Max. Mach operating speed	.86
Range (NBAA, IFR, 5 pax)	3,265 nm
FAA certified altitude	49,000 ft

The Challenger 604 has longer range than its predecessor and retains the line's coveted wide cabin. *Bombardier*

Falcon 900B/900EX

By the end of the 1970s it became apparent that the Canadair (later Bombardier) Challenger's widebody fuselage was becoming wildly popular with executive jet frequent fliers. Dassault realized that in the Falcon 50 it had the advanced, supercritical wing that could support a widebody fuselage and be competitive with the Challenger. The result was the Falcon 900 introduced in 1984. It delivered everything it promised in the cabin but turned out to be slightly underpowered, having to really struggle for altitude at high weights beyond 35,000 feet.

To improve climb performance, Dassault re-engined the Garrett (later AlliedSignal) TFE731-5A-powered 900 in 1991 with the improved TFE731-5B that has a thrust of 4,750 pounds, giving the airplane a total increase in thrust of 750 pounds and a 2-percent improvement in fuel efficiency. The modest thrust increase did such wonders for climb performance that

The Bombardier Special Edition is the Regional Jet airliner with a corporate interior. *Bombardier*

The Falcon 50EX interior. It hasn't had to change much since the Falcon 50's introduction in 1977 to remain enticing. The carpet is an example of the opportunities to personalize interiors. *Dassault Falcon Jet*

Dassault offered a retrofit to turn 900s already produced into 900Bs.

At its maximum takeoff weight of 45,500 pounds, the 900B can take off from a 5,000-foot runway and climb straight to 39,000 feet in 26 minutes. With five passengers and three crew it has a range of 4,000 nm with NBAA IFR reserves. And like the Falcon 50, it has excellent short field capabilities because of the low takeoff and landing speeds allowed by its leading edge slats and double slotted Fowler flaps.

The cabin is a triumph of design. The Falcon 900B is 40 percent lighter than the Gulfstream IV, yet not only can it fly almost as far almost as fast, but it has a cabin that is wider, offers a touch more headroom, and is as functional. Standard configuration is a three-zone layout consisting of a forward lounge, mid-section dining-conference area, and an aft lounge that converts into a private bedroom. Two lavatories (forward and

The Falcon 50EX, equipped with more powerful engines than the 50, can fly the same missions at Mach .80, compared to Mach .75, and has a longer reach at Mach. 75. *Dassault Falcon Jet*

aft) are an option for owners who don't want the occupants of the private bedroom disturbed by the other passengers and crew. A full service galley is standard, and all the usual entertainment and business communications equipment is available.

In the cockpit the 900B retains the 900's very capable but early generation Honeywell SPZ 8000 avionics suite and analog engine gauges.

The 900B was very well received, but Dassault perceived it could achieve additional sales with a slightly longer range version that could equal or exceed the G-VT's 4,200-nm range, to be offered concurrently with the 900B. The result was the Falcon 900EX, which entered service in November 1996.

The 900EX is equipped with AlliedSignal TFE731-60 engines rated at 5,000 pounds of thrust each, which give the EX a total increase in thrust of 750 pounds. It carries an additional 1,830 pounds of fuel and has a maximum takeoff weight of 48,500 pounds, up by 3,000 pounds from the 900B. The increased power gives the 900EX a range of 4,500 nm with eight passengers and NBAA IFR reserves and otherwise similar performance to the 900B. The cabin of the two aircraft is identical.

Dassault took the opportunity to upgrade the 900EX's cockpit, replacing the 900B's early generation Honeywell glass cockpit with a state-of-the-art Honeywell Primus 2000 avionics suite, including an electronic engine instrument display. The engines are auto-throttle equipped.

An outstanding portrait of the Falcon family. From top to bottom, 900EX, 900B, 2000, and 50EX. *Dassault Falcon Jet*

FALCON 900B/900EX VITAL STATISTICS

	900B	900EX
Powerplants (3)	AlliedSignal TFE731-5B	AlliedSignal TFE731-40
Thrust per engine	4,750 lbs	5,000 lbs
Passengers (typical)	12	12
Max. takeoff weight	45,500 lbs	48,500 lbs
Max. useful load	22,650 lbs	18,125 lbs
Max. Mach operating speed	.87	.84
Range (NBAA, IFR, 5 pax)	4,000 nm	4,500 nm
FAA certified altitude	51,000 ft	51,000 ft

Falcon 2000

With the Falcon 50, Dassault had a competitive narrow-body transcontinental airplane. With the 900/900B it had an outstanding widebody intercontinental airplane. What was missing from the product line was a widebody transcontinental airplane. The company filled the gap with the Falcon 2000, another cleverly conceived derivative design.

The 2000 designation suggests a link to the earlier Falcon 20 and 200, but this is only a marketing move prompted by the fact that the 2000 is a twin-engined airplane. It is, in fact a derivative of the Falcon 900B, with two engines instead of three, a slightly shorter cabin, and a much lower price.

Powered by two CFE738-1-1B engines rated at 5,918 pounds of thrust each, the Falcon 2000 has a 3,000 nm range at normal cruise of Mach .80 with eight passengers and a crew of three. Its reach in long-range cruise is 3,125 nm. Taking off at maximum

The 50EX shares its Collins Pro Line 4-equipped cockpit design with the Falcon 2000. The three engine displays (center) are Sextant Avionique LCD EIEDs. *Dassault Falcon Jet*

Right
The Falcon 900EX has a range of 4,500 nm and the most advanced avionics. *Dassault Falcon Jet*

Standing nearly 25 feet off the ground, the Falcon 900B's tail contains the mid-mounted horizontal stabilizer and the S-duct intake for the number two engine. *Geza Szurovy*

The Falcon 900 series super-luxurious widebody cabin. Behind the camera is an additional lounge that converts to a private bedroom. *Dassault Falcon Jet*

takeoff weight, it can climb directly to 41,000 feet in only 24 minutes.

The cabin is as luxurious as that of the 900 series but slightly shorter, providing room for a two-lounge configuration and an additional row of seats.

In the cockpit is a Collins Pro Line 4 EFIS avionics suite and three-screen Sextant Avionique EID that displays engine information. The package is the same as the one on the Falcon 50EX.

It is fair to say that in developing its current line of executive jets no company has taken as much advantage of a basic design as Dassault has of the superb Falcon 50.

FALCON 2000 VITAL STATISTICS	
Powerplants (2)	CFE738-1-1B
Thrust per engine	5,918 lbs
Passengers (typical)	10 to 12
Max. takeoff weight	35,800 lbs
Max. useful load	15,265 lbs
Max. Mach operating speed	.85
Range (NBAA, IFR, 5 pax)	3,125 nm
FAA certified altitude	47,000 ft

Gulfstream G-IV

Gulfstream was riding high through the 1980s with the G-III, but it was ripe for one major improvement to greatly enhance its performance. Its low bypass Spey engines were much thirstier and noisier than the more modern high bypass alternatives that were becoming the norm. Eastbound nonstop trans-Atlantic flights were routine for the G-III, but bucking the headwinds westbound meant a fuel stop more often than not. And its high noise level was beginning to hinder its operations, requiring special reduced thrust takeoff procedures as new noise regulations came into effect at certain noise sensitive airports.

So even while G-III sales soared, Gulfstream set to work on an improved model, the Gulfstream IV. It was equipped with two high bypass Rolls-Royce Tay engines, which were much more fuel efficient and quieter than the Speys and also had slightly higher thrust. Its wing design was further refined; the cabin was further enlarged, and the airplane got a state-of-the-art Honeywell SPZ 8000 glass cockpit and full authority digital engine controls (FADEC). The G-IV

One of the more unusual uses of an executive jet. A Falcon 900B arrives at Tswalu Game Reserve's private landing strip. Tswalu is South Africa's largest private game reserve dedicated to saving the desert black rhino. *Geza Szurovy*

was introduced in 1987 as the replacement for the G-III. Its big performance improvement was an increase in range from 3,691 to 4,220 nm, which it could accomplish at its normal cruise speed of Mach .80 compared to the G-III's lower long-range cruise speed of Mach .77 over the shorter distance.

There have been two significant refinements to the G-IV, an increase in various operating weights and an enhancement of the flight management system. The G-IV SP (Special Performance), introduced in 1992 as an upgraded model that replaced the original G-IV, had its maximum landing weight by increased 7,500 pounds to 66,000 pounds. Landings are rougher on the landing gear than takeoffs, hence maximum landing weights on large aircraft are usually well below maximum takeoff weights, restricting fuel loads on short flights to be within landing weight limits on arrival.

The SP's higher landing weight significantly enhances the airplane's mission capabilities allowing for a long series of short hops with high fuel loads. The

A Falcon 900EX turning final to an airport that never sees an airliner. *Dassault Falcon Jet*

The Falcon 2000 widebody transcontinental jet over Manhattan. *Dassault Falcon Jet*

SP's maximum takeoff weight also went up slightly to 74,600 pounds, and maximum payload (passengers and baggage) increased from 4,000 to 6,500 pounds. These results were accomplished by reinforcing some of the wings' ribs and stringers and beefing up the landing gear to take the extra load.

Following the debut of the G IV-SP, the Honeywell FMS was also upgraded to the SPZ 8400, notably expanding system memory and enhancing various functions and symbology.

The G-IV series has proved to be the best selling Gulfstream to date, with over 350 delivered by mid-1998 and a healthy order backlog. This is an outstanding accomplishment in view of the cost cutting business climate in which the G-IV was introduced. Downsizing

was about to make its big splash, and costly business jets, frequently viewed by outsiders as excessive perks, were an easy target, especially the "royal barges." But with downsizing came globalization, a concept for which the G-IV was tailor-made.

Coinciding with the need for corporations to become more efficient was the collapse of political barriers to capitalism that triggered an unprecedented growth in international business. The trend continues unabated as the whole world rushes to embrace the benefits of the free market. Roaming the globe is no longer an exotic option for senior executives but an everyday necessity to beat the competition. For the Fortune 100 league the G-IV with its long reach, comfortable cabin, and scheduling flexibility proved

The Gulfstream IV-SP's cockpit, equipped with the Honeywell SPZ 8400 avionics suite. The two central screens display engine and systems information. *Gulfstream*

The Gulfstream IV-SP's cabin outfitted for intercontinental travel. The aft suite (shown in the foreground) converts to a comfortable private bedroom with direct access to the aft bathroom. In this configuration, owners usually also opt for a second forward lavatory. *Gulfstream*

to be an eminently justifiable way to go. In fact, for a handful of companies, globalization has created a need for an even longer range large corporate jet, prompting Gulfstream to develop a new stablemate of the G-IV, the ultra-long-range G-V.

The G-IV's Honeywell flight management system presents on six 8x8-inch CRT displays not only all the flight, navigation, and engine information but also status reports and schematic depictions of a variety of the aircraft's systems, such as the hydraulic system, fuel system, electrical system, and all the checklists.

Initial climb rates of as much as 5,000 feet per minute can be achieved in a maximum performance climb at low density altitudes. A G-IV SP set 31 time-to-climb world records in 3 record categories, including a climb to 49,200 feet (15 kilometers) in 15 minutes, 25 seconds (on official record flights with appropriate preparation an aircraft may exceed its maximum certified altitude). In normal line operations under standard conditions a fully loaded G-IV can reach its initial cruising altitude of 41,000 feet in about 20 minutes, with a steep climb to 45,000 shortly thereafter.

The greatest luxury in a corporate jet's cabin is space. While the Gulfstream IV's cabin is not as wide as the Challenger's, it is decadently spacious and is longer. To counter the Challenger's advantage, the G-IV SP has more space than the G-IV, thanks to a judicious redesign of the interior paneling. The SP's "Wide Inside" interior provides an extra 6 inches of cabin width at seat level and an additional 7 to 11 inches at shoulder height.

Custom design is the norm for Gulfstream interiors, and the options seem limitless. Every conceivable kind of wood, leather, fabric, and exotic metal is available for interior finishing. The seating arrangements and cabin layout come in a wide array of choices. Club seating, sideways-facing three-person couches, and the four-place conference table are all popular elements of the typical cabin. In most configurations, six sleeping berths can be made up from the seats, including a double bed from the four-seat conference area.

Customers may choose to have the galley in the back, up front, or in the middle if they wish. The most exquisite dinnerware and glassware may be selected and adorned with the customer's corporate

The Gulfstream IV-SP, equipped with high bypass, FADEC-operated Rolls-Royce Tay engines, pushed the G-III's 3,600-nm reach to 4,200 nm. *Gulfstream*

logo or personal moniker. The bathroom may be in the back or up front or in both locations, one for the crew and one for the passengers. Some customers elect to have a partitioned off aft seating area that also serves as a private bedroom with the seats converting into a comfortable double bed. A shower in the bathroom is also an option.

In addition passengers are pampered by the airplane's sophisticated environmental control systems.

Dual cabin pressurization systems keep cabin altitude to only 6,500 feet at the G-IV's maximum certified altitude of 45,000 feet. This cabin altitude is about 1,500 feet lower than the typical cabin altitude on most other jets. Fresh air is constantly drawn into the circulation system instead of reliance on recirculated air, and the powerful Rolls-Royce Tay engines allow the airplane's air conditioner to operate normally during takeoff even at maximum takeoff weight under the most extreme conditions.

The CEO flying a Gulfstream does not have to feel out of touch during those comfortable hours aloft. With an optional satellite communications system pioneered for business jet use by Gulfstream, fax capability, and a computer workstation, the airplane may be wired for around-the-clock worldwide communications.

Typical destination pairs within comfortable G-IV range are New York–Zurich, Tokyo–Moscow, Seattle–London, Miami–Buenos Aires, Chicago–Honolulu, and Los Angeles–Tahiti. But the G-IV's long reach makes it a versatile international performer in more ways than one. Its ability to fly many short hops without refueling is also highly valued, especially in those parts of the world where refueling services are not always available and the price of fuel may vary enormously from country to country. A fully fueled G-IV SP can leave Brussels for Berlin, Prague, Warsaw, and Moscow and return to Brussels without the need to refuel. Another itinerary within its reach on one fuel load is Singapore, Bangkok, Saigon, Brunei, Jakarta, and a return to Singapore.

GULFSTREAM G-IV SP
VITAL STATISTICS

Powerplants	Rolls-Royce Tay MK 611-8
Thrust per engine	13,850 lbs
Passengers (typical)	12 to 14
Max. takeoff weight	74,600 lbs
Max. useful load	32,500 lbs
Max. Mach operating speed	.88
Range (NBAA, IFR, 8 pax)	4,220 nm
FAA certified altitude	45,000 ft

The Gulfstream IV's Rolls-Royce Tay turbofans deliver more power and significant fuel burn and noise emission improvements over the Speys found on the earlier Gulfstream IIs and IIIs. *Paul Bowen*

5

ULTRA-LONG-REACH, ULTRA COMFORT

Ultra-long-range executive jets are aircraft with a range in excess of 6,000 nm and a price in 1998 of approximately $37 million and up. The ultra-long-range executive jet is a relatively new phenomenon. It has a small niche market that developed as a response to the increased globalization of business. A specific catalyst was the dramatic expansion of business travel to the Far East. By the early 1990s many Asian locations were routinely reachable nonstop by the airliners even from the U.S. East Coast, but no business jet could cross the Pacific without a fuel stop.

The Gulfstream V ultra-long-range executive jet in its element, roaming the world with a range of 6,500 nm. The G-V won the 1997 Collier Trophy for pioneering ultra-long range executive-jet travel. *Gulfstream*

This changed in 1997 when the Gulfstream V became the first business jet to fly nonstop from Tokyo to New York on a record-breaking, round-the-world flight.

There are only two manufacturers of traditional executive jets in the ultra-long-haul market. Gulfstream was the first to roll the dice with the development of the Gulfstream V which entered service in 1997. About a year later it got head-to-head competition from the Bombardier Global Express. So far the two super executive jets have defied the skeptics who questioned the viability of the ultra-long-haul market. Brisk sales have resulted in order backlogs of several years, and both manufacturers are well on the way to passing the break-even point for these high risk projects.

Encouraged by the high interest in the ultra-long-haul business jet market, the two top airline makers of the world, Boeing and Airbus, have also gotten into the act with corporate versions of two of the most popular airliners. Boeing has made available a derivative of the 737-700 as the Boeing Business Jet. Airbus has introduced a business edition of the A319, the A319 Corporate Jet. These aircraft have slightly less range and are slower than the G-V and the Global Express but provide unsurpassed cabin space with room for as many as 50 passengers in executive comfort.

The ultra-long-range executive jet is without a doubt the king of business jets—until some imaginative entrepreneur builds a supersonic business jet, a matter not of *if* but *when*.

Gulfstream V

The Gulfstream V is by far Gulfstream's highest performance and most extravagant creation to date. Its maximum range of 6,500 nm represents a whopping 50 percent increase over the reach of the Gulfstream IV-SP, the previous long-range title holder among executive jets. In less than half an hour even a fully loaded G-V can climb above most airline traffic to its initial cruising altitude of 41,000 feet to be on its way undisturbed via the most direct route.

The G-V is powered by two BMW Rolls-Royce BR710 engines that deliver 14,750 pounds of thrust each. Though both names are best known for their automotive reputation, BMW Rolls-Royce is an exciting new joint venture company headquartered outside Berlin that marks BMW's return to the aviation engine industry after a long absence and links it to Rolls-Royce, one of the world's premiere jet engine makers.

The G-V achieves its NBAA IFR maximum range of 6,500 nm with eight passengers at Mach .80. This reach makes such nonstop flights as Los Angeles–London and New York–Tokyo a reality, as the G-V demonstrated on a record-breaking, round-the-world tour in April 1997 when it became the first business jet to fly each leg nonstop. Maximum cruise speed of the G-V is Mach .87, and its service ceiling is 51,000 feet.

The high lift wing and powerful, fuel efficient engines allow the G-V to operate from relatively short runways, in high field elevations, and in hot and humid conditions to the limits of its range.

The G-V's twenty-first-century cockpit resembles a TV studio or the work station of a Wall Street trader.

Gulfstream V an hour out of London's Stansted Airport on the Los Angeles–London first leg of its historic record-breaking round-the-world flight in April 1997. This was the first time an executive jet flew nonstop between Los Angeles and London. On a subsequent leg, the G-V flew nonstop from Tokyo to New York, also a first for a business jet. *Geza Szurovy*

The first G-V's wing takes shape at Northrop Grumman's Vought facility in Dallas, Texas. Vought is a risk-sharing partner with Gulfstream in the G-V. Risk sharing with sub-assembly manufacturers has become a common practice in new aircraft development. *Vought*

Every display but one is a CRT or LED screen. There are six large main displays and eight smaller ones, all integrated into the airplane's Honeywell SPZ-8500 Flight Management System.

Operating the system has many similarities to working on a battery of personal computers. Call up a function on a screen with a few keystrokes, enter your commands, and monitor your progress. There is even a disk drive to load your flight plan into the flight management system. Or, better still, you can get the flight plan automatically zapped onboard via the G-V's satellite communications system.

The management of engine power is also highly automated. Like the G-IV, the G-V has full authority

digital engine control (FADEC), which means that digital commands sent aft by wires from the cockpit control the two massively powerful BMW Rolls-Royce engines instead of mechanical linkages.

The cabin resembles a luxury apartment. Soft, warm light splashes richly over the soothing couches and club chairs. A wide selection of leather and plush fabric is available for the interior. One client specified iguana skin for part of the upholstery. Many varieties of exotic woods may be selected for the cabinetry and paneling, including blonde pickled beech, Brazilian sapele mahogany, bird's eye maple, and walnut burl. The wood is finished in over a dozen layers of urethane enamel and hand-polished to a mirror-like sheen that would do justice to the most opulent luxury yacht. The G-V's signature oval Gulfstream windows, six on each side, flood the cabin

The Bombardier Global Express gives new meaning to "flight deck" with its spacious layout and Honeywell Primus 2000 avionics suite. *Bombardier*

Left
With an initial rate of climb of over 4,000 feet per minute, the Gulfstream V can reach its lofty cruising altitude of 41,000 feet in no time. *Gulfstream*

Bombardier Global Express ultra-long-range executive jet displaying its advanced wing. With a range of 6,700 nm at Mach .80 it is the longest range executive jet. At Mach .88 it can cruise 5,000 nm. *Bombardier*

with light and provide the most panoramic view to be found in any executive jet.

G-V buyers also have great flexibility in customizing interior configurations. Aircraft regularly flown 14- to 15-hour nonstop flights that require a relief crew (such as the New York–Tokyo run) may be equipped with a crew rest area and a second lavatory up front. A shower is another option. The galley may be in the front or back, and the cabin may be divided into compartments or left in an open layout. A South American client, who is trading in her G-IV for a G-V to put all her European residences within nonstop reach of Buenos Aires, is having a private bedroom installed. Interiors can also be designed to be convertible.

About three-quarters of Gulfstream operators are North American, mostly Fortune 500 companies, but the company sees new sales evenly split between U.S. and overseas customers. If sales trends are any indication, the G-V is well on its way to meeting expectations.

GULFSTREAM V VITAL STATISTICS	
Powerplants	BMW Rolls-Royce BR710
Thrust per engine	14,750 lbs
Passengers	13 to 15
Max. takeoff weight	89,000 lbs
Max. useful load	42,600 lbs
Max. Mach operating speed	Mach .90
Long-range cruise	Mach .80
High-speed cruise	Mach .87
Range (NBAA, IFR, 8 pax, 4 crew)	6,500 nm
FAA certified altitude	51,000 ft

Right
An unusual formation shot of Bombardier's two new aircraft which entered service in the late 1990s. Learjet 45 (foreground) and Global Express. *Paul Bowen*

Bombardier Global Express

The Bombardier Global Express upholds the Challenger's tradition for having the largest cabin in its class and charts a new path with its exceptional performance. Bombardier faced a tough marketing challenge with the Global Express because it was a year behind its arch rival, the Gulfstream V, in introducing the airplane into service. Good things, however, are worth waiting for.

The Global Express is a slightly larger airplane with a slightly higher useful load and range than the G-V, yet it is powered by the same engines at the same speeds at similar cruise power settings. This advantage in performance is made possible by its advanced technology wing that was designed from scratch. It features a wing sweep of 35 degrees, a third generation transonic airfoil that has a comparatively flat top surface, and a double crank trailing edge. Airline-style leading edge

Bombardier Global Express on the assembly line at the company's Downsview, Ontario, facility. *Bombardier*

and trailing edge high lift devices provide low-speed control and low takeoff and landing speeds that enable the Global Express to use runways as short as 5,550 feet at maximum takeoff weight.

Bombardier's engineers made extensive use of Computational Fluid Dynamics analysis and computer-aided three-dimensional interactive application (CATIA) techniques to design the airframe. In addition to optimizing the wing for the airplane's long-range missions, they also did an outstanding job of controlling drag around the engine pylons.

The FADEC-operated BMW Rolls-Royce BR710 engines of the Global Express deliver 14,690 pounds of thrust each and are well suited to the airplane's advanced airframe. With eight onboard plus four crew members the Global Express can fly 6,700 nm with NBAA IFR reserves cruising at Mach .80. At Mach .85 its reach with a similar payload is 6,500 nm, and in high-speed cruise at Mach .88 its reach is 5,000 nm. This capability enables it to fly nonstop between such city pairs as New York–Shanghai, Sydney–Los Angeles, Hong Kong–Madrid, and London–Santiago.

The cockpit is a space age flight deck, equipped with a Honeywell Primus 2000 XP avionics suite that includes a Laseref III inertial reference system and TCAS. Six 8x7-inch flat-screen displays are neatly aligned to provide EFIS/EICAS information.

From the passengers' perspective one of the most attractive features of the Global Express is its ultra-spacious cabin. Its diameter is wider by a foot than the G-V and the floor width is 1.5 feet greater, giving the cabin space an even greater sense of being a room than is the case with the already generous dimensions of the G-V. The cabin is also the longest among executive jets (with the exception of the airline conversions), leaving extra generous space for a crew rest area, a welcome feature considering that the airplane is expected to routinely make nonstop flights of over 14 hours.

Typical seating configuration is for 12 passengers, but the Global Express can carry as many as 19 in a high density executive layout. The sky's the limit in the number of alternatives for configuring and finishing the cabin's interior.

The Global Express made its international debut in June 1997 with a flight from Wichita, Kansas, to

The Global Express has plenty of headroom. *Bombardier*

The Global Express' three-zone cabin is wide enough to accommodate a twin bed at an angle (aft) and an office complete with executive desk. *Bombardier*

The Global Express on final approach during its first flight. Note the leading edge slats and double slotted Fowler flaps. *Bombardier*

Paris Le Bourget under the command of Bombardier's Vice President for flight test, Pete Reynolds. The flight demonstrated the ability of the ultra-long-range airplane to make shorter trips at high speed. The 4,184-nm distance, which amounted to only 62 percent of the Global Express' range, was flown at Mach .85 all the way and took 8 hours, 28 minutes. This time was 1 hour and 16 minutes less than it took a Bombardier Challenger 604 to make the same trip. Customer deliveries of the Global Express commenced in 1998.

BOMBARDIER GLOBAL EXPRESS VITAL STATISTICS

Powerplants	BMWRolls-Royce BR710
Thrust per engine	14,690 lbs
Passengers (typical)	8 to 19
Max. takeoff weight	93,500 lbs
Max. useful load	50,550 lbs
High-speed cruise	Mach .88
Range (NBAA, IFR, 8 pax, 4 crew)	6,700 nm
FAA certified altitude	51,000 ft

Boeing Business Jet

The Boeing Business Jet is an audacious attempt to steal some of the thunder from the Gulfstream V and the Bombardier Global Express, the two titans of the ultra-long-range corporate jet niche. A derivative of the Boeing 737-700, it has about three times the cabin space of the Global Express and aims to be not only the ultimate in executive transportation, but a mobile global headquarters or personal Air Force One.

With the increased globalization of business, when so much work is compartmentalized into a set of short term projects, there is a need for a larger number of company executives to travel together and work en route more efficiently than is possible on the airlines. It is this sub-niche of the ultra-long-range market that the Boeing Business Jet and the Airbus Corporate Jet seek to corner.

The Boeing Business Jet optimally carries 25 passengers in executive jet comfort as far as 6000 nm, which puts destination pairs such as Los Angeles–Tokyo and Geneva–Johannesburg in reach. With eight passengers, range can be stretched to 6,200 nm, but this falls short of the range with a similar passenger load of both the Gulfstream V and the Global Express and is flown at a lower cruise speed. With 50 onboard in first-class configuration, which still leaves room for an executive suite, its reach is 5,280 nm. The airplane's maximum cruising altitude is 41,000 feet, which keeps it among the rest of the airliners, and its maximum cruise speed is Mach .82.

Gulfstream first announced it was considering building an ultra long range corporate jet at the annual NBAA convention in 1989, and officially launched the program at the 1992 Farnborough Airshow. The result was the G-V, shown here in its element. *Gulfstream*

The cabin configuration options provide for multiple conference rooms, offices, private bedrooms, and even an entire private apartment within a complex of conference rooms and lounges. An exercise room and spa can also be arranged.

Thanks to the economies of scale that come with belonging to the family of the most successful airliner, the Boeing Business Jet costs approximately as much as the G-V and the Global Express. It is, however, more expensive to operate unless it is flown at near full passenger capacity when it does become competitive on a passenger-mile basis.

How great the demand for the airplane will be remains to be seen, but there is little downside for Boeing in building them to order, given the Business Jet's ability to piggyback off the success of the 737 program. One thing is for sure though. No production executive jet will be able to match the luxury available on either the Boeing Business Jet or the Airbus Corporate Jet.

Artist's impression of the Boeing Business Jet, a conversion of the Boeing 737-700, which can carry up to 25 passengers in executive comfort and up to 50 in first-class comfort. With 8 passengers its range is 6,200 nm, with 25 it is 5,825 nm, and with 50 it is 5,270 nm. *Boeing*

BOEING BUSINESS JET VITAL STATISTICS

Powerplants (2)	CFM 56-7B
Passengers (typical)	8-50
Max. takeoff weight	171,000 lbs
Max. useful load	77,000 lbs
High-speed cruise	Mach .82
Range (NBAA, IFR, 8 pax, 4 crew)	6,200 nm
FAA certified altitude	41,000 ft

Airbus A319 Corporate Jet

After Boeing announced the Boeing Business Jet, could Airbus have been far behind? Sure enough, in June 1997 the company announced the Airbus A319 Corporate Jet, which provides the largest cabin of any corporate aircraft available as a production airplane. What Airbus has cleverly done is to speedily convert an existing jetliner to corporate configuration. The airplane is the 124-passenger A319 that was introduced into service in April 1996.

Two major changes are incorporated into A319s destined for corporate use with first deliveries in 1999: a highly customizable executive interior and a modular expansion of fuel capacity to extend the aircraft's range up to 6,300 nm, which is commendable but falls somewhat short of both the Bombardier Global Express and the Gulfstream V. The fuel tank modules are put in place through the cargo container hold and can be quickly tailored in capacity to suit the fuel requirements of a particular mission.

The airplane's cockpit remains unchanged from the airliner edition. The systems are noteworthy for being the most high tech among civilian aircraft with fly-by-wire flight controls (and little side sticks instead of traditional control columns) as well as FADEC.

A particularly attractive feature of the A319 Corporate Jet is that it is certified as a commercial airliner and can be easily converted back to standard airliner configuration, an option that makes the airplane much more marketable on resale.

The corporate Airbus (now a case where the company's plebeian name, chosen to curry favor with the traveling masses, is a marketing drawback) is intended to carry anywhere from 8 to 50 passengers. As can be imagined, the interior's degree of opulence is practically unlimited.

Like the Boeing Business Jet, the A319 Corporate Jet costs about as much as a Bombardier Global Express or a Gulfstream V but is more expensive to operate except when the number of passengers it is carrying approaches its full complement of 50. Like the Boeing Business Jet, its maximum cruise speed is Mach .82, and its maximum cruising altitude is 41,000 feet.

The G-V and its main competitor, the Global Express, share the same powerplants—two BMW Rolls-Royce BR710 turbofans. Pictured here is a G-V in flight. *Gulfstream*

AIRBUS A319 CORPORATE JET
VITAL STATISTICS

Powerplants	CFM 56 or Z2542
Passengers (typical)	8-50
High-speed cruise	Mach .82
Range NBAA IFR	6,300 nm
FAA certified altitude	41,000 ft

Index